PRAISE FOR *RISE ABOVE THE STORY*

"Karena has, in *Rise Above the Story*, not only written a book that is a wonderful read, but is one of great purpose. It's a beautiful gift to the millions of us who have labored under the impressions that have influenced our lives in challenging ways. Because of Karena's kind, compassionate, and caring nature, she has shared her own stories, and most importantly, her methods on how to rise above our stories. She shows us how to liberate ourselves from the grip of those experiences that all too often limit our chances to live life to the fullest. This book is a gift for which I am grateful and one that I will acquire in bulk to give to my friends, family, and fans. It is truly a gift of love."

—Mike Love, lead singer and lyricist of The Beach Boys

"In this extraordinarily candid book, Karena does more than dig deeply into her own story. She helps us understand how digging just as deeply into our own story can set us free. When you open *Rise Above the Story*, be prepared for a demanding journey. And be open to a fresh and joyful destination."

—Richard Celeste, former Governor of Ohio
and author of *In the Heart of It All*

"I've always said one of the most valuable things women do is share our histories and experiences. Occasionally, I hear a story that grabs ahold of me, and *Rise Above the Story* did just that. I was absorbed from the start. The book details the journey of a woman who goes through a hellish upbringing and, against all odds, not only survives, but soars. This book is a testament to the strength and resilience within each of us, and through her words, Karena Kilcoyne will guide you in overcoming your own obstacles. Prepare to be captivated, moved, and ultimately uplifted by a tale that reminds us that we are stronger than we think. Once you start, you won't be able to put the book down, and you'll be better for it."

—Suzi Weiss-Fischmann, author and OPI co-founder

"*Rise Above the Story* is packed with actionable insights along with compelling storytelling, all narrated by a wise, authentic, and relatable voice. Karena shares hard-won truths about the nature of trauma, recovery, and catharsis. Sharing her own empowering and heartbreaking story, she shines a light on a path to healing that will light the way for many."

—Andrea Miller, CEO and founder of YourTango.com,
host of the podcast *Open Relationships: Transforming*
Together*, and author of *Radical Acceptance

"How does your personal history define you today? A deeply insightful and encouraging blueprint for self-betterment, *Rise Above the Story* is an invitation to challenge your past, redefine your present, and reset your mindset for a kinder future."

—Leon Logothetis, author of *Go Be Kind*
and host of *The Kindness Diaries*

"It takes more than courage to transform a painful past into a flourishing future. It is Karena's open heart, loving nature, optimistic outlook, and the desire to help others heal that has turned her story of hurt and anguish to a guidebook for others to overcome their trauma."

—Jacqueline Lundquist, author, journalist, and filmmaker

"To the millions of people who endured childhood struggles, including me, Karena says, "it's ok." It's ok to share your story. It's ok to ask for help. It's ok to finally let it all go. *Rise Above the Story* is the guidebook we all need to acknowledge, release, and move beyond our limiting stories and find lasting emotional freedom. By sharing her own incredible story, Karena gives you the freedom and opportunity to reflect on your own personal path and PREVAIL!"

—**Todd Buchanan, President, World Financial Group**

"Yes, yes, yes! *Rise Above the Story* is a beautiful offering for anyone who has ever known the tender pain of trauma in their past. This book encourages us to understand that while it's important to honor and work through our past experiences and traumatic events, what matters most is knowing that we hold a part of us that is untouched by anything in our past. I absolutely loved this offering from Karena Kilcoyne."

—**Katie Silcox, *New York Times* bestselling author and founder of the Shakti School**

RISE
ABOVE
THE
STORY

RISE ABOVE THE STORY

Free Yourself from Past Trauma
and Create the Life You Want

KARENA KILCOYNE

 BenBella Books, Inc.
Dallas, TX

Rise Above the Story copyright © 2024 by Karena Kilcoyne, LLC

The cover is inspired by the Hindu festival of Holi, the celebration of color, spring, and love. It also commemorates the victory of good over evil and releasing one's inhibitions to find joy, compassion, and forgiveness.

 BenBella Books, Inc.
10440 N. Central Expressway, Suite 800
Dallas, TX 75231
benbellabooks.com
Send feedback to feedback@benbellabooks.com

BenBella is a federally registered trademark.

Printed in the United States of America
10 9 8 7 6 5 4 3 2 1

Library of Congress Control Number: 2023026945
ISBN (hardcover) 9781637743904
ISBN (electronic) 9781637743911

Editing by Rachel Phares
Copyediting by Lyric Dodson
Proofreading by Jenny Bridges and Denise Pangia
Text design and composition by Aaron Edmiston
Cover design by Karena Kilcoyne and Morgan Carr
Printed by Lake Book Manufacturing

Special discounts for bulk sales are available.
Please contact bulkorders@benbellabooks.com.

David

Your love is boundless.

Thank you for believing in me even when I didn't believe in myself.

A lifetime with you is not enough.

Finn

I look for you in my dreams.

I would not have written this book without you.

Irwin

Thank you, my furry love, for lying at my feet through thousands of words and countless drafts.

I am better because of you and your unconditional love.

My barn having burned down, I can now see the moon.

—Mizuta Masahide

CONTENTS

PART 3: RISING ABOVE THE STORY

INTRODUCTION

The morning was crisp and bright, as if it were meant for someone else. I peeked through my bedroom window and watched Dad get into the passenger side of the car. He had nothing packed, no bags. *How strange*, I thought, *to be leaving for years and not take anything except the clothes he was wearing.*

As he pulled the car door shut, my heart lurched forward in unison. I pressed my nose to the window, praying I could see his face. I couldn't. Would he look the same in two years? And wasn't that too long to be locked up for changing some car titles? Was rolling back a few odometers really worth a girl losing her dad? I wanted to throw my arms around him and give him the hug I'd denied him minutes before. I bolted down the hallway and out the front door. When I got outside, his car was already up the street.

"Wait! Dad, don't go. Please don't go." Dust blew up from the road until his car vanished from sight.

. . . .

My story took shape in a scrappy, shuttered steel town in northeastern Ohio. And while the gray skies and rusted-out steel plants painted a swath of gloom for the lot of us, it was the shame and abandonment festering in my makeshift home that crafted my decades-long story of unworthiness.

My mother tried, unsuccessfully, to give me away at birth. My father was sentenced to a federal penitentiary when I was twelve, requiring me to forfeit my childhood and care for my siblings and our mentally unstable mother, who'd spend days at a time despondent in bed. Most of my pain was forged in the shame of how I grew up and what I had to do to ensure we all survived.

I went to bed many nights with my stomach empty but my mind filled with dreams of crisp fish sticks and lemon jelly doughnuts. When hunger overwhelmed me, I searched drawers, pockets, and under cushions for loose change. What I scrounged together, I collected in a brown paper lunch bag and then rode my bike to the closest market. I left my young siblings alone, praying the entire time I was gone that nothing bad would happen to them.

As I walked up and down the store aisles, I mentally added up the total of the items in the cart: milk, bread, American cheese, tomato soup. At the checkout counter, I prayed no one got in line behind me. It took a long time to count out the correct change and hand it to the cashier, who then recounted it with a banker's diligence. With every plop of a coin into the register, I grew relieved we were closer to the total but mortified that people were watching me pay with lint-covered change.

When the loose change was gone, I honed strong survival skills asking strangers for money and doing without water and electricity. As traumatizing as the material deprivation was, it was my mother's and father's emotional abandonment that fractured me into a maven hellbent on survival and an ashamed little girl unworthy of love.

My parents' inability to construct a childhood for me made me an outcast. When I couldn't relate to those my age who were happy and carefree, I withdrew. My emotionally absent parents, and the shame I felt because of their neglect, kept me from developing self-esteem, joy, and a true sense of belonging.

Through my teens and twenties, I existed in a gray-skied mental landscape that repeatedly recounted the stories I believed about myself.

No one wanted me.

I would never be good enough.

I could never be happy.

Even though I lived inside those stories, it was my fear of failure and, even more so, my fear of becoming my parents that propelled me into a seemingly successful life. Knowing education was my ticket out of poverty, I put myself through law school, graduating when I was twenty-four. Shortly before graduation, my mother died, leaving me to adopt my nine-year-old brother. I defended millionaires and accused murderers, all while trying to parent my brother, doubting my own self-worth, and suffering from anxiety. To the outside world, I was the picture of well-adjusted success, but my overwhelming shame made me feel anything but. Nothing in my life felt on course or meaningful because my life choices were filtered through my story of unworthiness, sorrow, and abandonment.

As a result, I routinely settled for less. I made choices based on fear and what others would think of me. I married a man even though our relationship lacked passion and deep love. I suffered through bouts of reeling panic, which offered the occasional terrifying jolt to my otherwise numbed-out existence. I slept with other men just to feel something, anything other than the dull, gnawing pain of my seemingly hollow life.

But no matter who I married, kissed, or slept with, my story of abandonment kept me chained to a loveless existence. I didn't know how to love anyone, let alone myself. And without that innate love, my story of worthlessness bound me up so tightly I didn't know the real me. I only knew the scared, shameful, little me—the twelve-year-old girl who was left in the dust. The one who constantly craved validation and acceptance. The one who was never enough.

There were moments throughout my adult life when I believed that professional success would redeem me. That passing two state bar exams, representing death row inmates, and defending big corporate executives would finally give me the sense of worth and belonging I so desperately craved. But there wasn't enough external validation in the world to heal my deepest, oldest wounds. And as my false story of shame and abandonment grew larger, my life grew smaller.

There had been moments over the years when I dabbled with the idea of healing—I bought a few books, did energy work, and saw a therapist. Then I'd convince myself that I was fine and didn't need help. But after a devastating breakup in my mid-thirties (which you'll hear all about later), I admitted I wasn't fine. That was when I first acknowledged my story. I admitted that it was keeping me from joy and real love. I vacillated there, in the space between acknowledging and healing, for a few more years until my beloved dog Finn died.

For years, I'd shamefully hidden all my dark memories and stuffed every corresponding emotion. I'd refused to grieve my childhood trauma because part of me, that maven hellbent on survival, insisted on perfectionism, pushing, and excelling. But when Finn—who loved every imperfect piece of me—died, I couldn't contain the tsunami of grief. My abject sorrow for Finn opened the floodgates, and swells of unresolved emotions rolled through me relentlessly.

Consciously experiencing them for the first time, I wept uncontrollably. There was grief for my lost childhood. Rage and resentment for my mother. Disappointment and sadness for my father. A deep longing for true happiness. And then, there was my desperate desire to finally belong, not only to this world but to something meaningful and extraordinary, perhaps something Divine.

As the waves of my old, trapped emotions dissipated, I tasted the sweet, airy lightness of emotional freedom. I glimpsed what my life could be without fear and shame. Joy was within reach, but I had work to do. There was so much more of my past that needed to be uncovered, processed, and resolved. My life had been defined by stories of shame, but I wondered—who could I be without those stories? Who would I be without my past defining my present?

I was finally ready to rise above my story.

To begin my healing, I dove deep into traditional therapy and inner child work. I then moved on to more integrative methods, such as past life regressions, breath and energy work, and anything else that would help me release my deepest rage and grief. Early in the process I realized I had to be completely honest about the stories I'd written for myself. I had to get clear on how I'd let them define me and why I clung to them even though they caused me so much pain. Ultimately, that self-awareness, that state of pure mindfulness, was the key that unlocked my healing.

Unraveling decades' worth of emotional malnourishment and releasing the shame that fueled my story would take everything I had. But I was determined to rise. The deeper I went into myself and my pain and the broader my healing became, the more I realized I wasn't alone in my storytelling or my suffering.

Countless people are shackled to their sad, untrue stories: parents, siblings, teachers, therapists, religious leaders, and friends. Rock stars, movie stars, and athletes, too—no one goes unscathed. From time to time, they all fall prey to that limiting voice inside them that says things like:

Who are you to be a singer, actor, painter, or playwright?

You think you can excel at that? You've failed at everything you've ever tried.

How could you possibly make a difference? Nobody cares what you think.

During my career as a criminal defense attorney, I witnessed first-hand how my clients' stories negatively impacted their lives. Stories of shame and unworthiness led to drug addiction, crimes of passion, gang affiliation, and financial fraud. Many of my clients deserved more than the stories they believed about themselves. Even my own father, whose abandonment took me years to forgive, had a story of abandonment that he never rose above. It took me a long time to see his frailty. I didn't have the emotional tools to truly forgive him until I healed myself. Once we learn how to rise above our own story, we gain the wisdom and compassion to forgive others and help them rise above their stories, too.

What I know to be true after decades of suffering and finding a path toward healing is that the past doesn't define you.

You do.

I also know that if I could do it—if I could rise above my story—you can, too. And that's why I wrote this book—to share how I did it.

I went here, there, and everywhere seeking the formula to heal myself. There were many opinions and offerings. Was I depressed? Yes. Was I lost? Absolutely. Was I anxious? Without a doubt. But not all that was offered worked. Some of it was too shallow to reach my deepest wounds, and some of it was too broad to offer tangible comfort. But what did resonate, what did help me rise above my story, is in this book—every raw, beautiful detail.

And while I am frank and vulnerable with you in the pages of this book, I have changed the names and circumstances surrounding events to protect the privacy of those involved. The essence of the story, and the feelings and emotions evoked, are to the best of my recollection. I offer all of this and what flourishes on these pages as a safe passage for your healing.

There are countless books and resources out there about success, persistence, healing your inner child, trauma, and coping with depression. But there isn't one with this universal formula of resilience, inspiration, and empowerment. Not one that breaks open the complexity of a human being's fear of truly thriving as their truest self with such a poetic yet doable simplicity. Not one that will teach you how to rise above your story.

If you've been living in the past, afraid of the future, or ashamed of who you are, this book is for you.

If you're living a small life, one limited by the constructs of the stories you believe about yourself, keep reading.

If you're wondering why you feel so empty when you have so much, you're not alone.

If you think everyone has the answers but you, stay tuned.

If you drive yourself with fear and perfectionism instead of compassion and joy, you'll switch gears with me here in the pages of this book.

If, because of your trauma, you're making safe choices and doing the "right thing" at the cost of your health and happiness, I'm thrilled you're here, and you will be, too.

So often we carry our untrue stories with us as days turn into weeks, months, and then years. Before we realize it, we've relinquished our power and allowed the stories of our unworthiness to steer us into apathy or, even worse, misery. Some of us know we're living in the shallow end of life. We promise ourselves that we'll change, but we don't. And before we know it, years have gone by and here we are, still bottled up with emotional dis-ease and quite possibly suffering from physical disease.

What would your life look like if you finally forwent your fear, uncovered the real you, and rose above your story? I'll tell you that for me it meant emotional freedom. Once I let go of the narratives that were holding me back, I was no longer chained to memories that drowned me in falsehood. I developed a keen awareness of my negative default settings and learned to reset them to full-throttle joy. Everyone experiences trauma and limiting stories at some point. But it is our soul's purpose to find emotional freedom and live a big, limitless life.

It is for us to rise above our story.

Who could you be if you rose above your story? Perhaps someone who's filled with unfettered joy? Someone who laughs and plays with abandon? A mindful aware being who embraces all of who they are with unconditional love? A fearless foot soldier of humanity who has the wisdom and grace to create a bespoke life of abundance? Sounds pretty amazing, right? It absolutely is.

While it's empowering to know that we can rise above our story, how do we actually do it? This book is divided into three sections, each one guiding you to rise as I share my own stories and experiences as well as many different healing methods that can help you untangle even your most gnarled stories. We'll also walk through deep inquiry, enlightening lessons, and journal prompts that will help you ultimately rise above your story.

Our journey will unfold like this:

Part 1: This is where you will acknowledge your story. You'll cultivate self-awareness toward healing and get honest about the stories you're telling yourself and how they've limited you, your life, and your dreams. By the time we get to the end of this section, you'll be excitedly wondering who you could be if you left your story behind.

Part 2: Here's where we untangle your story. I'll ask how you got tangled up in your story in the first place and how it took control of your life. By sharing some of my most traumatic stories, I'll show you how you, too, can extract your deepest truth. Doing this may require some spiritual tools that will unearth your deepest fear and trauma. But don't worry. I'll share with you what worked for me and how unearthing those old traumas will set you free once and for all.

Part 3: This is where we ultimately rise above our story. Our journey blossoms here! I'll show you how you can let your stories of the past serve you. We'll unearth the lessons and wisdom found in the traumas we all endure and do a deep dive into self-love. I'll show you how to embrace every part of yourself, even the parts you've cast away in shame.

But before we get started, there's something you must accept unconditionally: if you want to rise above your story, you must be willing to
do the work yourself. Rising above won't happen if you wait for others
to fix you, want you, love you, or rescue you. Because the truth is this:
the only person who can rescue you is you.

There is not one person in the world who will understand the depth
and breadth of what you've been through. No one will feel the texture
of your pain like you do. And quite frankly, it's unfair to put the onus of
healing your pain on someone else. This is not to say that having a support system of people who care about you isn't helpful. It absolutely is.
But the inner work required to rise above your story is yours to do alone.

I know this may feel overwhelming. We all, at some point in our
lives, believe that we'll meet *the one* who will magically make us happy
and heal all of our wounds. We desperately seek a soulmate, hoping that
falling in love will magically make us whole. It won't. Listen, I'm all
about magic and destiny when it comes to love, but even (insert your
dream person here) carrying a Universe of stardust can't lift you up out
of your own story.

It's impossible.

No one else can do the work of rising but you. While it may seem
daunting, it's actually quite empowering to know that you and you alone
are in charge of your life and your destiny. If you want to rise above your
story, you must actually want to. (Check! You wouldn't be here with me
in the pages of this book if you didn't want to heal.) You must also be
willing to do the work yourself, for yourself. Again, this can certainly
be done with the help of a good therapist and the love and support of
friends and family (and me!). But the work itself, the deep dive into the
dark past and what can feel like the endless search for the light, is for
you to do alone.

Nothing worthwhile comes easy, especially not something as transformative as developing self-awareness of your traumatic imprints and healing your most profound emotional wounds. But I have no doubt that you can do this, and I'll show you step by step what it takes to rise above. I'll also share the empowering tools you'll need to keep rising, because healing (and rising) is never a one and done. There will be a multitude of opportunities to rise above old triggers and new stories. With enough practice, you'll meet the challenge with resilience and grit. You will see rising above as an invitation to ascend higher—mentally, emotionally, and spiritually.

Rest assured that by the time you get to the end of this book, you will have found *the one*. You'll find that magical soulmate who loves every part of you.

You will find yourself.

It took me years to find myself and even longer to finally love the real me. But it was the greatest gift I've ever received. And I would never have felt that kind of love had I not disavowed the stories I believed about myself—especially those centered around my abandonment and worth. These days, I know I'm worthy of abundance and love, especially my own.

And that's what I want for you.

I have no doubt that the unconditional love we have for ourselves can change the world. By casting away our limiting stories and embracing the rich vibrance of our authentic selves, we can radiate loving energy into the world. Can you imagine a world where we all feel liberated despite our race, gender, sexual identity, or social or political circumstance?

That's exactly what will happen when we all rise above the story.

Part 1

. . . .

ACKNOWLEDGING THE STORY

It always seems impossible until it's done.
—**Nelson Mandela**

1

TRAUMA: THE ORIGIN OF THE STORY

We all have a story, or a hundred, don't we? Our minds buzz with those haunting narratives, convincing us that we're lost, unworthy, unloved, or unwanted. Some of us may even feel like imposters in our own lives. And more often than not, our stories are the byproduct of our trauma. Meaning, that as a result of our trauma, we subconsciously write a story about ourselves that keeps us confined to a small life. This is the brain's way of keeping us "safe." Before we dive into why the brain does this, let's get clear about trauma—the origin of our story.

While societal norms often neatly categorize trauma as big "T" trauma (war, violent crimes, natural disasters) or little "t" trauma (job loss, illness, divorce), for most of us, trauma is messy, with no definitive lines of demarcation. In reality, trauma's pain is as unique as the individual who experiences it. Depending on where trauma registers on your personal spectrum, your ability to process emotions, and whether you are more innately sensitive to the world around you, your pain may resonate even deeper.

In addition to the pain of the trauma itself, there is also the pain we endure when we write a story about ourselves as a result of the trauma. These stories are well-penned tales of shame, fear, and worthlessness that fuel our day-to-day existence, leaving our souls aching with loneliness.

If you're like me, maybe your trauma occurred early, like in the womb early. I sloshed around in a sea of confusion, absorbing the despair and shame of my nineteen-year-old mother, who, five years later, confirmed the story emblazoned on my DNA: *my own mother didn't want me.* Which is why, after giving birth to me, she left me at the hospital hoping that someone, anyone, would take me off her hands. When they didn't, she returned begrudgingly to reclaim me and settled back in with the abusive hustler she believed to be my father. The fact that she told me all this while sitting on the front stoop of our apartment building and sipping a whiskey sour hurt me just as much as the actual tale of her giving me up for adoption. I would come to learn that abandonment can actually strike harder if someone stays than if they go.

In the ideal world, the credits on that traumatic incident would've rolled right there on those dirty concrete steps, and my pain would have stayed tucked tightly away in 1977. Little five-year-old me would have shrugged off Mom's cocktail-fueled confession and skipped out to catch lightning bugs, knowing I was so much more than my mother's abandonment. But little me didn't know better. Instead, from that trauma, I wrote a story of abandonment, worthlessness, and shame. I replayed that story for decades, constantly finding reinforcement for its "truth" with every failed relationship, setback, and rejection, no matter how big or small.

Countless people write their stories in childhood, and it's easy to see why. Historically, we believed that experiencing trauma early in life resulted in less psychological injury than if the trauma happened later; however, more recent research has shown quite the opposite. It turns out that the younger we are when we experience trauma, the more significant and lasting the impact.[1] This makes sense considering that as early as the womb, we absorb our mother's stress and anxiety.[2] In fact, much of an adult's ability to modulate mood, control impulses, and effectively regulate anger is a result of their in utero environment.[3] If the mother is depressed or enduring great stress, the fetus's lifelong levels of dopamine and serotonin (the feel-good hormones) are negatively impacted.[4]

After birth, our minds are constantly seeking to make sense of what's happening around us despite not yet having the ability to speak and put our experiences into words. This makes any trauma experienced at that young age nearly impossible to reconcile. In the book he cowrote with Oprah Winfrey, *What Happened to You: Conversations on Trauma, Resilience, and Healing*, Dr. Bruce Perry discusses early life brain development and writes, "And because so much of the world is new when you're a baby, that's when your brain is most rapidly and actively making these new connections. The experiences in the first years of life are disproportionately powerful in shaping how your brain organizes."[5]

With our early brain formation and inability to process trauma, it's no wonder so few of us escape childhood unscathed. According to the Substance Abuse and Mental Health Services Administration, over two-thirds of children reported experiencing a traumatic event by the age of sixteen.[6]

Such traumatic events include:

- community or school violence
- witnessing or experiencing domestic violence
- national disasters or terrorism
- sexual exploitation
- sudden or violent loss of a loved one
- refugee or war experiences
- military family–related stressors, such as deployment, parental loss, or injury
- physical or sexual assault
- neglect
- serious accidents or life-threatening illness

While trauma occurring during formative years has a significant and lasting impact, there is no doubt that trauma can have significant repercussions at any age. The National Council for Mental Wellbeing reports that approximately 70 percent of adults in the United States (or 223.4 million people) have experienced trauma at least once in their lives and that "trauma is a risk factor in nearly all behavioral health and substance use disorders."[7] This is further supported by the council's report that over 90 percent of public behavioral health patients have experienced trauma.[8]

The long-term effects of trauma include post-traumatic stress disorder (PTSD). According to the National Institute of Mental Health (NIMH), approximately 6.8 percent of all adults in the United States will develop PTSD in their lifetime.[9] NIMH also reports that women are more than twice as likely as men to be affected by PTSD.

As disturbing as these statistics are, my gut feeling is that the number of people suffering from trauma is much higher than reported. Undoubtedly there are droves of people who don't discuss their trauma due to emotional suppression and shame. We are unquestionably a traumatized bunch, and it is our brain's subconscious, emotional interpretation of our trauma—or what I call "our story"—that dangles us incessantly over a canyon of soul-numbing fear.

LET'S SUM IT UP

Trauma comes in many forms, each manifesting varying degrees of physical, mental, and emotional harm. And while experiencing childhood trauma can be particularly devastating, experiencing trauma at any age can alter the course of our lives. When we experience trauma, our subconscious mind writes a story about who we are because of the trauma. Oftentimes, these untrue narratives tell us we're unworthy and unlovable and fill us with shame. We may all experience trauma differently, but there is a common denominator for the lot of us: trauma is the origin of our story.

2

· · · · · · · ·

YOUR BRAIN IS A
MASTER STORYTELLER

W hile this book is a spiritual, emotional, and mental deep
dive into healing, we do need to cover just a bit of science. Now that we know trauma is the origin of our story,
it's important to understand how our brain develops, how it interacts
with our nervous system, and why, in response to trauma, it writes our
shame-filled stories. So, whether your story was written in childhood or
later in life, understanding how the brain functions is the foundation of
our healing.

Stay with me and you'll see why.

HOW THE BRAIN DEVELOPS

While there are many illustrations and explanations of the brain and its development, the hand model of the brain created by Dr. Daniel Siegel, a clinical professor of psychiatry at the UCLA School of Medicine, offers us an ingenious, visual representation.[10]

To understand Dr. Siegel's model, open your right hand in the upward position, as if you're taking an oath. Your wrist mimics the spinal column. Now fold your thumb in toward your palm and fold your four fingers over top of your thumb.

The base of your palm represents the brainstem, sometimes called the reptilian brain. This is the oldest evolutionary part of the human brain (300 million years old). It's also the first area of our brain to develop, taking shape while we're still in the womb. Throughout our lives, the reptilian brain receives and processes internal information from the body and external information from the world around us. In turn, it regulates the automatic survival functions of the body such as our heart rate, breathing, temperature control, and arousal. It also controls our fight, flight, or freeze response, which is our body's physiological reaction to potential danger.[11] There's no high-level thinking in the brainstem. It's all autopilot regulation.

Now peel your fingers away from your palm and expose your thumb. The thumb represents the limbic brain, which evolved 200 million years ago.[12] This area of the brain is the second to develop. It's present at birth and continues to develop through the teen years. The limbic brain is where we cultivate emotional connections with ourselves and others.[13] Along with the reptilian brain, it assesses whether situations are good or bad, safe or dangerous. And when there's a real or perceived threat to our safety, the limbic brain works with the reptilian brain and the nervous system (which we'll discuss in a bit) to engage our fight, flight, or freeze response.[14]

These two parts of the brain make up what we refer to as the subconscious mind because much of what they control is automatic or routine. They assess information based on past experiences, forming conclusions about how to respond by comparing new information to previous, similar circumstances.[15] Any resulting physical response to those situations, such as fight or flight, is automatic. This means that when we experience something that resembles an old trauma, the emotional brain might shift us into survival mode, even if it's objectively unwarranted.

The third and final area of the brain to develop is the cortex, also called the neocortex or the cognitive brain. You can identify the cortex in Dr. Siegel's hand model of the brain by folding your fingers back down so your fingertips are once again resting against your thumb.[16] Your wrapped fingers represent the cortex. The space between your middle knuckle and first knuckle is the frontal cortex, and the area from your first knuckles to your fingernails is the prefrontal cortex. This is where our conscious mind and sense of self reside.[17] It's also where we practice reasoning and judgment and process information before acting impulsively.[18] While prefrontal cortex development is rapid during the first two years of life,[19] full maturation doesn't occur until our mid-twenties.[20]

With the reptilian and limbic areas of the brain developing first, we see that the brain prioritizes survival over the more complex functions of the cognitive brain, such as conscious thought and reflective reasoning. Even after full development, the brain will default to autopilot, allowing the reptilian and limbic areas to run the show with routines and habits. It takes mindfulness and self-awareness to shift out of lower brain subconsciousness and into higher brain conscious thinking.

Now that we've identified the three areas of the brain—reptilian, limbic, and cortex—let's simplify our discussion even more. In his groundbreaking book, *The Body Keeps the Score: Brain, Mind, and Body in the Healing of Trauma*, Dr. Bessel van der Kolk discusses the significant interaction and interdependence between the reptilian and limbic brains and, thus, collectively refers to them as "the emotional brain."[21] For ease of discussion and clarity throughout this book, I will do the same. To further simplify our discussion, I will refer to the cortex, frontal cortex, and prefrontal cortex as the "thinking brain" throughout this book.

IDEAL BRAIN DEVELOPMENT VERSUS REALITY

In ideal brain development and functioning, the emotional and thinking brains will integrate in harmony.[22] This means that information would be sent freely between the two areas of the brain, with the thinking brain processing questionable information before action is automatically taken by the emotional brain.

In the best-case scenario, the thinking brain would develop awareness, compassion, and empathy for itself and others. And with enough time and practice, the thinking brain would also nurture strong response flexibility, which is that seemingly elusive power to control your emotions even after someone pushes all your buttons.

But let's be realistic. Who has the perfect early childhood and trauma-free life required to ensure ideal brain development and function?

Is that even possible? There are countless factors that may negatively affect brain formation, such as nutrition and genetics. And, as we've learned, the emotional health of our caregiver is also a pivotal factor in brain development.

Dr. Gabor Maté, a celebrated speaker and best-selling author in the fields of stress, addiction, and childhood development, writes about the crucial nature of a caregiver's role in his book, *The Myth of Normal: Trauma, Illness, and Healing in a Toxic Culture*. He writes, "[A] child's early emotional interactions with their nurturing caregiver(s) exert the primary influence on how the brain is programmed—again, the unconscious comes first, followed later by things like intellect . . . Given this order of operations, children's sense of security, trust in the world, interrelationships with others, and, above all, connection to their authentic emotions hinge on the consistent availability of *attuned*, *non-stressed*, and *emotionally reliable* caregivers. The more stressed or distracted the latter, the shakier the emotional architecture of the child's mind will be."[23]

This is all to say that if we aren't properly nurtured and soothed by our caregiver during early life, we'll struggle with trust and intimacy in our relationships. And more importantly, we won't form an authentic connection with ourselves. Without this connection, we won't trust our emotions or learn how to soothe ourselves, which are two key characteristics needed for emotional health throughout our lives.

External circumstances, such as how we're raised and by whom, undoubtedly affect brain development and whether the emotional and thinking brains integrate harmoniously. These early life circumstances go a long way in explaining how we process trauma and the stories we write because of our trauma.

THE NERVOUS SYSTEM

Along with the brain, the nervous system also plays a key role in the stories we write about our trauma. Often called the command center of the body, the nervous system sends signals from the brain through the body.[24] There are two main parts of the nervous system: the central nervous system and the peripheral nervous system. The peripheral nervous system is composed of the somatic and autonomic nervous systems. While the somatic controls the voluntary movement of our muscles, it also sends the information from our senses to the brain.[25] The autonomic oversees the subconscious or involuntary actions of the body needed to survive, such as breathing and heart rate.[26]

Diving just a bit deeper into the autonomic nervous system, we see that it is made up of two parts—the sympathetic and the parasympathetic nervous systems. When the emotional brain senses danger or experiences trauma, the sympathetic nervous system runs the show, engaging our fight-or-flight response. It shifts us into survival mode and floods our body with adrenaline and cortisol—two hormones associated with stress in the body—that enable us to stay and face the danger or turn around and flee. This automatic stress response may cause an increase in heart rate and blood pressure, dilated pupils, clammy palms, loss of memory, heightened senses, and an inability to feel pain until after the traumatic incident has ended.[27]

When we can't fight or flee, we might experience the freeze or disassociation stress response. Often, we shift into freeze mode when we're too young to escape or the trauma is too harrowing to endure.[28] To lessen the physical and mental pain of the trauma, the brain releases endorphins that enable us to survive the situation. Trauma researchers have suggested that freezing during a traumatic experience is one of the most significant predictors for later developing PTSD.[29]

When the threat is over and we feel safe, the parasympathetic nervous system kicks into gear and calms us down, returning us to homeostasis.[30] When we feel safe, we'll relax, sleep, eat, poop, and play. In this mode, our body also does its routine cellular cleanup, keeping us healthy. Conversely this means that if you're stressed and continually operating in fight or flight—for instance, if you're enduring ongoing trauma—your body is not able to effectively relax, sleep, and heal.

A well-tuned, regulated nervous system will fluctuate between sympathetic and parasympathetic modes quite efficiently. In fact, we're meant to have a flexible, resilient stress response. When we can shift from stress to calm throughout the day, our nervous system is well regulated.

On the other hand, a dysregulated nervous system is problematic. Dysregulation occurs when our stress response receptors are overstimulated or sensitized due to unpredictable, prolonged, or developmental (childhood) trauma.[31] Hypersensitization of the nervous system can occur at any age due to ongoing trauma, but continual childhood trauma, such as violence, scarcity, or abandonment, have a particularly destructive impact. In his book *What Happened to You*, Dr. Bruce Perry chillingly describes children who grow up internalizing the trauma of a distressed, dysfunctional household as "incubated in terror."[32]

Severe dysregulation of the nervous system can last for decades if not treated properly. This means that after enduring a traumatic and chaotic childhood, we can remain in fight, flight, or freeze overdrive well into adulthood. When this happens, we are conditioned for survival and not much more. In his book, *Mindsight: The New Science of Personal Transformation*, Dr. Daniel Siegel, who created the hand model of the brain we discussed earlier, writes, "When we are in survival mode our reactivity makes it quite challenging, if not outright impossible, to be open and receptive to others."[33] When this happens, everything and anything can feel like a threat.

In my deepest, most entangled years of pain, I called my perpetual state of fear "Chicken Little mode." I was constantly afraid, believing that the sky was falling around me all the time. Maybe you've experienced that overwhelming sense of anxiety, too? Or maybe, like me, you've felt unsafe in the world, particularly in relationships? Living in this perpetual state of fear can cause panic instead of connection. It can also cause you to expect the worst, act clingy, pick fights, and constantly question people's intentions.

Much like fight or flight, the freeze response can also remain in overdrive and continue well into adulthood, causing us to zone out and not fully invest in ourselves or life. We may tiptoe around the fringe of our relationships, subconsciously terrified of intimacy. We may also become people pleasers, avoiding conflict at all cost.

Living in stress response overdrive takes a tremendous toll on our mental and emotional health. In addition, a hypervigilant nervous system can lead to various physical diseases, which we'll discuss in greater detail later in the book.

PUTTING IT ALL TOGETHER— HOW THE EMOTIONAL BRAIN PUTS OUT FAKE NEWS

So how do the brain and the nervous system work together to create our limiting stories? Imagine your brain is a newsroom that's constantly receiving information and determining what's factual and newsworthy. Ideally, your emotional brain would gather questionable information and send it upstairs to the thinking brain for processing. The thinking brain would then logically analyze it, consider the source of the information, and determine how and when the information should be reported.

Now imagine that the reporters working in the emotional brain department go rogue and refuse to send any information upstairs to the thinking brain. Instead, they hoard all the information, processing it themselves based on past emotional experiences instead of logic, and without verifying whether sources of the information are credible. The emotional brain reporters filter information through a muddied lens of past traumatic news, causing them to sense danger at every turn.

These reporters then write a news story, the undercurrent of which is doom and gloom. The article is anything but objective. Instead, it reeks of subjectivity—I mean, it's literally fake news. In a state of panic, they ascertain that the only way to ensure safety is a complete emotional lockdown. Without fact-checking the story, the reporters signal the rest of the workers (the nervous system) to go on high alert. The workers flood the network (your body) with breaking news alerts of the story, blaring an annoying, high-pitched beep and issuing warnings on all fronts. *Danger! Danger!* The fight, flight, or freeze response is engaged. Overly stimulated by the alarms, the emotional brain begins to believe its own fake news and eases into the perceived security of its chaotic, closed-off existence, making way for a dysregulated nervous system.

By now, the emotional brain has completely disengaged from the smart guys upstairs in the thinking brain. Believing that it knows how to protect you and keep you safe, the emotional brain will isolate you from your true self. To do this effectively, it will use its best weapons: fear, doubt, shame, and uncertainty. It will run discouraging messages that prevent you from following your dreams, finding peace, and being vulnerable. Your emotional brain chatter will sound something like this:

Don't say that. No one will like it.

Or . . .

Don't do that. You'll make a fool of yourself.

Or . . .

Don't fall for that person. They'll never love you back.

Or . . .

Don't forgive that person. They deserve your hatred and resentment.

What better way to ensure your survival, especially after being traumatized by what is supposed to be love, than to keep you as far away from love as possible? To ensure it's doing its job, the emotional brain will write a story of unworthiness so convincing you will shun vulnerability and intimacy. So, while you might be "safe," you also live a small life, foregoing love, joy, and deep connection. We're also lonely, sad, and entrenched in a cycle of limitation and scarcity.

When we're in this pattern, breaking free can feel undoable. But it's not. We just have to do it one step at a time. Our ultimate goal in healing is to create awareness around our trauma and the story our emotional brain wrote about it. We must also level up our thinking game by processing the suppressed emotions trapped in the emotional brain and sending them upstairs to the thinking brain. This integration will bring us inner peace and harmony.

Rising above our story means rising above the stories created in the emotional brain. Rising above means we thrive in the sweet spot of conscious awareness and mindfulness, where we no longer allow the emotional brain to reactively determine our mood or worthiness. We'll no longer let the past define who we are.

This may seem impossible, but it's not. I promise, we will get there. All you need at this point is an awareness that trauma is the origin of your story and an understanding that your emotional brain, to protect you, harnessed the pain of your trauma and wrote a false story that you're unworthy of love and happiness. The rest, dear reader, will unfold in due time.

DON'T BE ASHAMED—WE'RE ALL STORYTELLERS

Breaking out of old patterns can seem daunting, I know. To make this leap feel more like a step, I want to remind you that you're not alone in the stories you tell yourself. Everyone has a story—presidents, bakers, models, CEOs, rock stars, artists, singers, dancers, dog groomers, and bartenders alike. Because our emotional brain subconsciously writes our stories, *anyone* who has a brain and has experienced trauma can have a story about how their trauma defined them.

But here's the irony: Even though we all have a story, and our stories often have uncanny parallels, they don't bring us together. In fact, it's quite the opposite. Our storytelling isolates us.

Society has conditioned us to hide ourselves—to disguise our pain, angst, and trauma—and put on a façade. When asked how we are, most of us respond with a programmed, "I'm fine." I don't know about you, but when I say, "I'm fine," 99 percent of the time, I'm anything but. Societal and cultural norms have shifted us into hiding the truth of what we experience and who we think we are because of it.

And they've done this using shame.

I grew up in the "shame on you" generation. Everything was shameful. Got a C on a chemistry test? Shame on you. Kissed another girl's boyfriend? Shame on you. Wrecked your first car? Shame on you. So many of us carry that shame deep into adulthood, where it plays on repeat in our brains. Didn't get the big job? Had an affair? Got a divorce? Shame, shame, and more shame. But here's the danger in carrying around all that shame: It will kill your dreams with a hot, slow burn as each aspiration shrivels inside you like a raisin in the sun. It will also silence your spirit and maliciously reinforce every limiting story you tell yourself.

When I first started writing about rising above our stories and sharing publicly that my father went to a federal penitentiary, a friend of mine told me that his father had gone to prison, too. Part of me couldn't believe it. This guy is a go-getter. A professional unicorn. A loving husband. A tremendous father. But then, part of me could believe it. We're taught to hide our pain because showing our wounds is exposing our weakness. Instead, we bottle it up and live in shame. But we all have the power to free ourselves from the shackles of shame. All we have to do is speak our truth and tell our stories. We must share what has happened to us and what we falsely believe about ourselves because of it. That is how we will regain our power.

One of the most crucial things you must know in this journey is that you are not alone in writing and reliving your old, limiting stories. Every single one of us has a story. But it's those of us who cultivate self-awareness and acknowledge our stories who will ultimately rise above these false narratives.

LET'S SUM IT UP

The brain is made up of what I'll call the "emotional brain"—the reptilian and limbic regions—and the cortex, or what I'll call the "thinking brain." Our emotional brain controls the automatic bodily functions we need to survive, such as breathing. The thinking brain, on the other hand, is the conscious part of the brain. It's where we develop critical thinking and reasoning skills.

When the emotional brain senses danger or experiences trauma, it will, along with the sympathetic nervous system, ignite the fight, flight, or freeze response. If we endure ongoing or developmental trauma, our nervous system can get stuck in fight, flight, or freeze, also called dysregulation.

Worried for our survival in the face of trauma, our emotional brain will craft a story to keep us safe. It's likely one of shame, abandonment, and unworthiness that keeps us in a state of fear. As it turns out, this story doesn't keep us safe at all. Instead, it creates a false life of limitation and scarcity, causing us to question our worthiness over and over again. Who are we to be happy? To be loved? To be emotionally free? These are the thoughts that overtake our inner landscape while our body continues to reel from nervous system dysregulation.

We can shift out of this debilitating pattern if we foster self-awareness around our trauma and our story. When we do this, we shift our storied thoughts from the emotional brain to the thinking brain, and we see through reasoning and compassion that we're not alone in our suffering. With this harmonious integration of the two parts of our brain, we also accept that we have nothing to be ashamed of. Everyone who has a brain and has experienced trauma can write a limiting story for themselves.

But if we develop self-awareness and rise above our story, we can live a big, meaningful life.

. . . .

NOW IT'S YOUR TURN

In the pages of this book, I share my traumas and previously shameful stories. Being vulnerable about my stories and shame was one of the most powerful ways I healed myself, and I'm certain it will help you, too. These "Now It's Your Turn" sections will include journal prompts geared toward unearthing your pain and releasing your shame. During this process, trust that you are safe and loved.

It is never easy to dive into the past, yet it is exactly what we must do if we are to heal ourselves. Everyone's healing journey is different and exquisite in its own right. Some of us might work through one chapter and the corresponding journal prompts several times before moving on to the next chapter. Or, we might return to certain chapters again and again if we feel there is more pain to unearth. Others may meditate, pray, find comfort in a friend, or talk with a therapist as they move through the pages of this book. There is no right or wrong way to heal. The only common thread for all of us is that we must walk through the darkness to get to the light. And we will do it together.

Here's all you need to do in these sections:

- Keep a designated journal for answering these questions. It's insightful to go back and examine your emotional evolution as you heal.
- Get cozy and comfy as you work through the journal prompts. Choosing a space where you feel safe to be vulnerable is crucial.

- Turn off your phone and avoid distractions. Tending to the deep, wounded part of you requires your undivided time and attention.

Now, let's get going! We're going on a trip through your brain. This may sound intimidating, I know. But don't worry. This is where we ignite our self-awareness. By surveying our mental landscape, we can begin to differentiate who we think we are versus who we really are. And trust me, very often they are nothing alike.

Imagine you're riding in an open-air Jeep. You're traversing the landscape as if you're on safari. You see open, spacious beauty on the left and a few dark corners on the right. The air and light are familiar, but the road leads to unknown territory. You aren't scared though. You're curious. Adventurous. Self-assured. You know that whatever lies ahead is manageable. There is no obstacle between you and the truth you seek.

Now write down the first thing that comes to mind when reading the following questions.

How was the physical, mental, and emotional health of your parents or caretakers?

Did you feel emotionally connected to and physically soothed by your parents or caregivers? Why or why not?

Did you experience childhood trauma such as abuse, scarcity, or abandonment?

Do you currently experience anxiety, depression, or panic?

Do you give yourself permission to relax? Is relaxing easy for you?

Are you high-strung? Do you find it difficult to sit still?

Do you sleep well?

Have you experienced heart palpitations, a quickened heart rate, or breathlessness?

Would you say that you're emotionally reactive; that is, do you anger easily or become impatient quickly?

How quickly can you relax and calm down after a stressful situation? Is it easy or challenging for you?

When you feel stressed, how do you soothe yourself?

Does intimacy scare you?

Do you connect with others easily?

Do you feel safe in relationships? Do you trust others easily?

Have you hidden your past traumas because you feel ashamed?

Do you feel that your story or your shame have caused you to remain in fight, flight, or freeze throughout your life?

Are you ready to let go of who you think you are and embrace who you really are?

The brain is a superpower that can be used for good or evil. It is when we step into self-awareness that we change how we see ourselves and the world. We can allow the emotional brain to dictate our mood, behavior, and outlook, or we can shift our mindset to higher thinking—to self-awareness, compassion, and love. It's a simple yet seismic shift in energy that begins with acknowledging your story.

Come along and I'll show you how it's done.

3

· · · · · · · ·

ACKNOWLEDGING YOUR STORY

After my divorce in my early thirties, and still carrying the story of abandonment and unworthiness written in my childhood, I set out on a path of soul-numbing destruction fueled by sex and booze. While many in my then circle refer to that period as "the good ol' days," for me it was the onset of my darkest time. My inner child was angry and rebellious. She was righteously pissed off for having to endure our parents' abuse and abandonment. She was outraged over her lost childhood. And the broken lens through which she viewed others, and especially herself, kept her from true connection.

During the day I was a successful white-collar criminal defense attorney representing millionaire executives. But by night, I was emotionally desperate and craving complete annihilation. On the nights when I wasn't out looking to get blackout drunk and have sex with emotionally unavailable men, I was home alone panicked and unable to sleep. Memories of the past kept me pacing compulsively through the hallways of my house.

One particular night, when the memories of my parents were scalding and thick, I stumbled to the bathroom and flipped on the light. Staring at myself in the mirror, I didn't recognize my form. My green eyes were hazy, like heat rising off a city street after a summer storm. My skin was tired and dull. My mouth was drawn into a frown that wouldn't budge. I twisted my thick blonde hair into a top knot and splashed cool water on my face. The fear and anger that raged inside me would not stop. I was terrified it might literally break my heart or cut off my airways, deciding I'd served enough of a sentence in this life.

The terror of losing myself once and for all rattled my soul. I knew something had to change or the weight of it all would surely kill me. And while I was, in present time, an adult chock-full of wretched panic, I also held a younger, rageful version of me locked in the past. In that moment, when my apathy toward life roared into full-blown anxiety, I questioned the limiting patterns I'd subconsciously placed on my life. Even as a successful professional, I felt unworthy of love, happiness, and of life itself. I rebelled against intimacy and denied myself the joy of belonging. Why was I doing this?

I began to see that the story I'd written for myself—the one that was supposed to keep me safe and tucked away from harm—was now causing me to reel in an abyss of misery. My negative, untrue story was now woven into the fiber of my being. And while the full unraveling of my story would take a few more years (and the death of my beloved dog Finn), it was that initial step toward acknowledging my story that began transforming my life from limitation to complete emotional freedom.

. . . .

Acknowledging our story is the first step in healing. If we want to ultimately rise above our old pain, we must, with unabashed mindfulness, choose to. We can no longer rely on the default settings of our emotional brain that do not serve us.

Acknowledging our story is done in two steps:

First, we identify the origin of our story, the traumatic event that caused the emotional brain to seek safety.

Second, we elevate our thoughts from the emotional brain to the thinking brain by using objective, factual language to describe our trauma and our story.

IDENTIFY THE ORIGIN OF YOUR STORY

Identifying the origin of your story—the trauma that fueled your limiting narrative—is a wholly unique endeavor. Some of us may be able to pinpoint with complete accuracy the one traumatic incident that started it all, while others, who endured ongoing, repetitive trauma, may feel as though they're lost in a labyrinth, unable to find their way out. That's exactly how I felt when I began the work of identifying my trauma. But with enough time and patience, I was able to sort through it. Here's what I came up with.

. . . .

Generationally locked in a rust belt city on the Ohio–Pennsylvania border, my people were a scrappy folk known for their pizza and Friday night lights. I was born to a couple whose own traumatic stories magnetized them to one another until the day my mother died at forty-four years old.

My parents had a passionate, violent relationship. Dad loved to tell the story of the first time Mom rode her bike past the used car lot he owned. He'd never seen anyone so beautiful. She'd say that she was attracted to his striking German good looks. Although I think it was the fact that he rescued her from her alcoholic father and abusive stepmother that really turned her on. At eighteen, she moved in with this short-tempered man, nine years her senior, and pretended, among other things, that she knew how to take care of a home.

Years later, their rage-induced fistfights left me hiding under my bed or ducking beside the couch. The number of broken dishes was only surpassed by the number of times Dad left us, slamming the door behind him. Mom would then sink into a deep depression, leaving me to subsist on Keebler Fudge Stripes cookies and cherry Kool-Aid. When hunger overcame her, she'd leave her bed just long enough to make a fried bologna sandwich, topped with a dollop of Miracle Whip, of which she'd give me half. And even though I hated Miracle Whip, I ate the sandwich because the warm bread and crisp meat comforted me like nothing else. That is, except for the love of Whoopsie, the bichon frisé puppy I'd had when I was six years old. We were only together for a few weeks before Mom gave him away.

When Dad returned home after an argument, I knew better than to jump off the couch and greet him. He and Mom would, of course, yell at one another and then there'd be a few slaps over the lipstick on his collar. Inevitably though, their anger would melt into passion. They'd retreat to the bedroom, where their moaning and groaning was only outdone by the rhythmic banging of the headboard against the wall. And once again, with this tumultuous reconciliation, everything was "fine" in my world.

I wrote my story about love during those days in our shabby basement apartment. I'd find temporary, heroic comfort in the return of a man who never laid a hand on me but beat my mother within a breath of her life on more than one occasion. With every return to their bed, they cemented in me the notion that love is fickle and untrustworthy. I caught on that people who leave don't love you, and those who stay probably don't either.

From early on I believed that my job was to be perfect and make everyone happy. This falsehood was spawned from my abandonment story. I subconsciously believed that if I did everything right, I'd make Mom and Dad happy. And in turn, they'd love me and, hopefully, never leave me.

It was a gargantuan story for a five-year-old, which was how old I was the first time I associated doing a perfect cartwheel with making Mom's eyes glisten with pride. Her hazel eyes were a well-calibrated barometer of her mood. When the bright green flecks of her irises were washed away by the deep, brown sea below, a storm was brewing in her that would surely result in a beating or at least some hair pulling. When I saw her eyes shifting from bright and calm to dark and muddy, I'd do cartwheels and act out Shel Silverstein poems. Whatever it took to keep her happy, I did it.

At just five years old, I had mastered the art of people pleasing.

"See, Mom, everything is great," I'd say, tightening my pigtails post cartwheel.

And there were moments over the next few years when it was great, well, *ish*. Great-*ish*. We'd ride around in our yellow convertible Cadillac tapping our fingers while the Bee Gees blared from eight-track tapes. The summer sun flushed my round Ukrainian cheeks as I blew bubbles with not one, but two pieces of Hubba Bubba bubble gum. We'd hop from store to store buying clothes and more eight-tracks with the stack of cash I'd taken from the freezer that morning. That's where Dad kept the money he made at his used car lot—in the freezer, wrapped in foil, and stuffed in Mrs. Paul's Fish Sticks boxes. He didn't believe in banks or writing checks. He also didn't believe in paying taxes, but that's a whole 'nother story.

"Don't tell Dad about the money we spent today," Mom would say.

I'd pop my bubble and double swear on Gloria Vanderbilt's life that I wouldn't say a word. But I didn't have to. Dad knew. He always knew. He'd taught me all about money. There were ones, fives, tens, and twenties. Mostly though there were fifties and hundreds. Lots of hundreds. After a while, there wasn't enough room in the freezer for all the money Dad made at the car lot. That's when we moved to the ranch-style house on the other side of town. It had a picket fence (which was the only idyllic thing about our life there) and the biggest yard I'd ever seen in all my eight years of living. I spent many evenings lying in the grass praying for peace and quiet in the house that Dad's hundreds bought.

But there were never enough hundreds to make Mom happy. Dad went to prison a few years after we moved to the ranch house, and Mom quickly spent all the money he left us. She sank into a bottomless pit of depression, sleeping for hours on end. She went days without bathing or eating. There wasn't anything to keep her alive except twelve-year-old me.

I had officially switched roles with my mother years earlier, when I was about six years old. Serving as her obligatory protector, I'd step in between her and Dad when they fought. But when Dad went to prison, protecting her no longer meant breaking up fistfights. It meant ensuring her survival. I cooked dinner—Campbell's tomato soup and grilled cheese sandwiches—while she lay in bed despondent. I asked strangers for money to help pay our electric bill. And when she was well enough to get out of bed, switching roles with her meant caring for my siblings while she went out for whiskey sours with strange men.

But no matter what I did or how much I tried, I could never be perfect enough to make Mom happy. As men came and went, I caught on that no one could ever fill the black hole that would eventually consume her. Through my college and law school years, I stayed in her orbit out of obligation. I gave her the money I earned because I worried for my siblings. Then I adopted my nine-year-old brother when she died because, well, I'd practically been his mother since the day he was born anyway.

The resulting story I wrote about relationships was defined by how I saw myself in the world (invisible) and what I believed I was worthy of (not much). And while my story led me to choose the wrong men (emotionally unavailable and often narcissistic), the most truthful story I wrote for myself was that physical abuse is not love. Watching my father beat my mother for something so insignificant as giving a neighbor a piece of birthday cake on one of our Corelle plates and then bearing my own mother's beatings until I was sixteen years old was enough for me to steer clear of physically abusive people. However, someone who was emotionally abusive or distant was not only free game but hotter than John Travolta in *Saturday Night Fever*.

My trauma, or the origin of my story, was recurring and long-term. Due to its pervasive nature, my story grew taller, wider, and more entangled with each passing day. It was a sophisticated web of deceit ensnaring me at every turn. It would take me years to untangle it and ultimately rise above it. But in order to heal, I had to pinpoint my first conscious memory of trauma—the origin of my story. And so I traveled back to that summer evening when I was five years old: The setting sun warming my cheeks. The concrete steps cooling the backs of my legs. Mom's hazel eyes and the scent of whiskey setting the stage for all the stories I'd write about myself—especially my abandonment.

. . . .

Going back in time and identifying our trauma is incredibly challenging. That's because our emotional brain is still trying to keep us safe. It will tell us our trauma was unbearable, so we must not get hurt again. It will say our emotional wounds are permanent and, therefore, we mustn't trust anyone. But remember, the emotional brain disseminates a lot of fake news. It will also resist our attempts to change our story around the trauma, making us feel afraid to even try. So how do we do it? This leads us to the second step in acknowledging our story.

ELEVATE YOUR THOUGHTS FROM THE EMOTIONAL BRAIN TO THE THINKING BRAIN

I know from personal experience that there can be an array of emotions surrounding trauma and the story we write about it. But to initiate the shift into self-awareness and acknowledge our story, we must elevate our thoughts from the emotional brain to the thinking brain. This disrupts the negative emotional patterns that have confined us. To do this, we must use objective, factual language to describe our trauma and our story.

HOW TO DESCRIBE YOUR TRAUMA

Early in my healing journey, I began meditating. I learned to detach emotionally from the thoughts floating in and out of my mind. Instead of reliving painful memories or planning a future to-do list, I stood as an observer or a witness to my thoughts, objectively acknowledging their presence but not engaging them with emotional commentary. When you make that shift, you're not judgmental of yourself or your thoughts. Instead, you step outside yourself and watch the thoughts as if they were playing on a movie screen. This allows for freedom and comfort in experiencing the memories that surface because you realize that they aren't happening to you. In fact, they aren't happening at all. They are memories. Thoughts that come and go. Emotions that flow in and out. The same idea can be beautifully applied to emotional healing and acknowledging your story.

When applying this concept to your trauma, describe the traumatic event only with the factual who, what, where, and when of what happened. This is not to say the emotional resonance of the trauma is not real or warranted. This factual description is to help elevate the thoughts around the event from your emotional brain to your thinking brain. We're establishing new patterns. We're choosing to send relevant information to the smart guys upstairs. The ones who analyze. Who reason. Who show compassion. Who don't jump to conclusions or keep doing the same thing repeatedly even though it doesn't work. Sorry, emotional brain. We're just calling it like it is.

When speaking objectively about your trauma, you create a space between yourself and what you experienced, hopefully lessening the trauma's emotional charge. From your new vantage point, you can see that your emotional brain wrote a story. And now, with the awareness you're cultivating, you also see that your story isn't keeping you safe at all. In fact, it's suffocating your very being.

HOW TO DESCRIBE YOUR STORY

The next step in shifting your story to the thinking brain is to change the language around your story. Like the foundation of any solid relationship, a healthy relationship with ourselves starts with honesty—full-throttle, eyes-wide-open, call-it-like-it-is honesty. We must be candid about the stories we've been telling ourselves. This does not mean we're judgmental and callous in our tone. It does not mean we're shameful or that we retell the story repeatedly. What it does mean is that we own up to the fact that we've written a limiting story for ourselves, one that's holding us back from love, success, and being our most amazing selves.

PUTTING IT ALL TOGETHER—HOW TO ACKNOWLEDGE YOUR STORY

Acknowledging your story can be challenging. We may have lived for years with an old mantra playing in our heads, making it feel impossible to change our emotional pattern. Just to get things churning for you, I'll go first. Based on what we learned above, acknowledging *my* story does *not* sound like this:

People always leave me. I am unworthy of anything good.

I am unworthy and unlovable. Even my own parents didn't want me.

I am ashamed that I grew up poor. No one can know this about me.

Instead, acknowledging my story sounds like this:

Because my mother tried to give me away at birth (factual), I falsely believed that I was unworthy and unlovable.

Because my father went to prison (factual), I told myself the untrue story that everyone would ultimately leave me and that I'm unworthy of happiness and love.

Because I grew up without necessities like food and hot water (factual), I was ashamed and mistakenly believed people would think less of me.

Again, the key is to acknowledge your trauma and your story with objective, factual language. There is no room here for victimhood (more on this later). Acknowledging happens when we embrace our inner strength and step into our power.

At first, this may feel like you're towing a car with your teeth. And since we're being completely honest here, you may find a certain amount of cruel comfort in retelling yourself your false narrative. Perhaps your story has subconsciously become your security blanket. Depending on the depth of your trauma and shame, holding onto your limiting story may feel oddly comforting. Better to hurt yourself than have someone else do it, right? I know. I've been there, too. It can be terrifying to put yourself out there, uninhibited by those untrue tales of the past. And anyone with a well-crafted story knows that being vulnerable is the very last thing we want to do.

But ask yourself this: Do you want to be in charge of your happiness? Do you want to purposefully steer your life toward joy, peace, and love? Or do you want to slog out the rest of your days relying on your fake-news emotional brain to direct your course? By acknowledging the stories you've been telling yourself, you will break free from your past and your old stories. You will break free of your negative emotional patterns. I can tell you that the freedom you'll experience after acknowledging your stories is nothing short of intoxicating.

LET'S SUM IT UP

Acknowledging your story is the first step in rising above it. And while it is challenging to change a habit, it is possible to shift your mindset. The first step in acknowledging your story is to identify its origin—the trauma that caused the emotional brain to write your story in the first place. Next, we elevate our thoughts from the emotional brain to the thinking brain by describing our trauma and our story with objective, factual language. We steer clear of victimized verbiage. This powerful shift in mindset and language will help us finally acknowledge those age-old limiting stories.

NOW IT'S YOUR TURN

This is where you get honest about all the stories you've written for yourself. Don't hold back here. It's not only likely but it's probable that you have multiple stories to acknowledge. Simply follow the prompts below for each story you have.

What you uncover below will become the map to where you go next. This is where your new life begins. So, light a candle, grab your journal, and close your eyes. Take a few deep breaths and ask for your truth to step up and be heard. Trust the thoughts and feelings that come up for you here. This is the doorway to your new life.

Remember, if we want to rise above the story, we must begin by acknowledging the story we're telling ourselves. We do this by:

1. Identifying the origin of our story, the trauma that caused the emotional brain to write our story.
2. Elevating the story from the emotional brain to the thinking brain by using objective, factual language to describe both our trauma and our story.

The following prompts are designed to shift you right into thinking brain mode, so follow them closely.

IDENTIFYING YOUR TRAUMA—THE ORIGIN OF YOUR STORY

Answer these prompts as factually and objectively as possible, meaning I'd like you to write about the trauma—the origin of your story—as though it happened to someone else. For now, let's keep the emotion surrounding the trauma out of the picture—we'll get deep into that later. In this exercise, we'll break down the facts of what happened—the who, what, where, and when of what occurred. You may have experienced more than one trauma. If so, answer the prompts for each traumatic experience. As we move through these exercises, be kind to yourself. This is the beginning of a beautiful journey.

What happened?

Who was involved?

How old were you?

Where were you?

ACKNOWLEDGING YOUR STORY

As a result of your trauma, what story have you been telling yourself? Use the prompts below to get you going in the right direction.

Because (write a factual statement about your trauma),
I told myself the untrue story that . . .

Because (write a factual statement about your trauma),
I falsely believed that . . .

*Because (write a factual statement about your trauma),
I've been living with a limiting story that . . .*

How long have you been telling yourself this story?

*How has this story made you feel? Sad? Unworthy?
Abandoned? Alone? Afraid? Timid? Be as clear and concise as
possible when identifying your emotions here.*

*Do you want to feel joy? Love? Intimacy? Success? Are you
ready to let the past go once and for all?*

Remember to work through as many stories as you have. There is no limit to the beautiful freedom you can create here. Once you've gone through these journal prompts for each of your stories, close your eyes and honor how you feel. You may feel tired, scared, uncertain, relieved, or excited. Everyone is different, and there is no right or wrong way to feel. This is only the first step in our healing journey. Be easy on yourself and honor the work you have done here. Also, trust that you will have a richer understanding at each step of our journey. I am so proud of you. Consider THIS a big hug from me.

We have a lot more to uncover. Let's keep going.

4

· · · · · · · · ·

HOW YOUR STORY SHAPES YOUR REALITY AND LIMITS YOUR LIFE

B y now you've acknowledged your story, and I'm proud of you. Admitting that you've been living inside a limiting story is, for many of us, the most difficult step in the healing journey. Developing self-awareness and being completely honest about your story is tremendous progress. Rest assured, you're well on your way to the promised land of emotional freedom. Bravo!

Now you're ready to develop even more self-awareness. True healing happens when we understand where we've been and how we got caught up in our pain for so long. This is why we're going to explore how your story shaped your reality and limited your life. When you understand this, you'll see how powerful our stories are and how insidiously they control us. You'll also see how your emotional brain kept you locked up in its fake-news reality. This is not to say that any of this is your fault. It most certainly is not. As Maya Angelou said, "Do the best you can until you know better. Then, when you know better, do better." Becoming mindful of how your emotional brain works and choosing self-awareness over your old stories is how we do better. Now let's dive in.

HOW OUR STORIES SHAPE OUR REALITY

When we live inside the construct of our stories, we see life through a distorted lens. Imagine you're looking at a picture of a beautiful beach on your phone. Cresting waves are glistening in the rich sunset. Dogs are romping happily in the sand. Then imagine zooming in and cropping the photo until all that remains is the bottom right-hand corner. It's part of the beach, but it's blurry and nearly unrecognizable. You no longer see the sunset or the sweet dogs.

This is exactly what happens when we live inside our story. We only see a tiny part of life—not the beauty or the joy. Instead, we zoom in on a small piece of life that doesn't make us happy. We no longer recognize where we are in the grand scheme; our perspective is so limited by our story that we can't fathom a bigger existence. And inside that wickedly shaped version of life, we feel limited in what we can do and who we can be.

I've shared the origin of my story with you. You know that as a result of my ongoing trauma, my story shaped my perspective on money, love, and relationships. With each new trauma, my stories constrained me even more. But the story I share next walloped me good and hard. By the time I got to the other side of this traumatizing experience, my reality had taken a new form—one that was even more confined. My dad might have been locked up in prison, but without a doubt, so was I.

. . . .

George and Betty's doors were buttoned up tight on that bleak winter day when I stood on the side of my house metamorphosing into a twelve-year-old hustler. I prayed they weren't home. But the smoke billowing from their chimney signaled that they were. They were my best option for cash, and they seemed nice enough, but I was afraid they hated me because my dad was in prison. I mean, what was there to like about the daughter of a felon anyway? I picked the skin off my chapped lips and prayed.

Please, God, let them say yes. I don't want to have to ask anyone else. And you know I can't go back home without money. Mom will beat me silly. Can you please help me? Please?

My stomach growled. And as if God gave me a little push, my right foot stepped out in front and then my left foot followed. I walked slowly through the yard and then across the street, my boots crunching the fresh snow. When I got to their door, I froze. I suddenly had to pee, which happened every time I got nervous. And then, even worse, my brain went blank. I forgot what I was going to say. How do you ask someone for money? We weren't *borrowing* it. I mean, we couldn't pay it back.

I couldn't do this. I turned around, and just as I stepped off the porch, George opened the door.

"Hi there, neighbor. Can I do somethin' for ya?"

I knocked my knees together trying to stop pee from running down my leg. *Please, God, please. Make me brave.*

I turned around and half-smiled. "Uh, I live across the street," I stammered, feeling stupid since he just called me "neighbor." "And, uh, well, my dad went away a while ago, and well—" My chin wobbled. Tears filled my eyes.

"I know, sweetie. That can't be easy. How's your mom?" He stepped back and opened the door a bit more. "Would you like to come in? It's awfully cold out there."

"No, that's okay." I backed up, suddenly scared of him. *Why was this guy inviting me into his house? Was he a pervert? I mean, no one could be this nice and normal, could they?*

I was just about to make a run for it when Betty came to the door wiping her hands on her apron.

"Hi there! I just made some cookies. Would you like to come in?"

They can't both be perverts, right?

"Okay, sure," I said, making my way through the door but keeping my distance from George.

Once inside, I took off my boots but left on my coat. A fire blazed in the family room. The smell of freshly baked chocolate chip cookies tickled my nose. Family photographs lined the walls leading to the kitchen. I stopped and studied George and Betty's wedding photo. They looked young and happy. We didn't have any family photos hanging on the walls of our house. I wondered if, along with the money, they'd give me some of theirs. A thick oak table was nestled in the corner of the kitchen. I stood in the doorway, plagued with guilt that I'd thought they were perverts. Actually, they were kind people who'd created a home full of warmth and love—exactly what I ached for in my own makeshift home.

"Please, sit," George said, pulling out a chair.

"How's your family, sweetie?" Betty asked. "Are you all adjusting without your dad at home?"

She set a plate of cookies in front of me.

Something about her—maybe it was the apron or her gold-rimmed glasses or her well-clipped fingernails—made me want to jump out of the chair, hug her tightly around the waist, and spill my guts about everything. Maybe they'd adopt me and hang my picture on the wall?

I snapped back into reality. I reached for a cookie and put it up to my nose. It was the best thing I'd ever smelled.

"Kind of, but Mom's sad a lot."

"I bet she is. Are you sad too?"

"Sometimes. It's hard when we don't have a lot of food." My cheeks flushed, not from the heat blowing through the radiator but from my candor.

"Are you hungry?" She opened a cabinet door. "What else can I make you?"

"I'm okay. I have to get home and watch my brother and sister. But my mom wanted me to ask you if we could, um—" I shoved the entire cookie in my mouth and looked out the window over the sink, avoiding her eyes. "Uh, borrow some money," I said, trying to hide my shame with loud chewing.

"Oh! You need some money?" George asked.

I used the few seconds of chewing and swallowing to devise the perfect reply.

"I mean, we *have* money." My leg jittered on the chair. "We just don't have any right *now*. It's Saturday, and the bank is closed, and, well, we need some groceries for the weekend."

I could not believe I just lied to them. I knew full well that Mom would never pay them back.

"Oh, well, yes of course," he said, pulling his wallet from his back pocket. "How much do you need?"

My mind quickly ran the options—ask for a little not to be greedy or ask for a lot since he seemed willing to give it.

"How about twenty?" he asked, handing me the bill. "Would that be enough to get you through?"

I smiled with relief at Andrew Jackson's face.

"Yes, sir. Thank you very much." I stood up and grabbed the money. "Thank you both." I walked backward out of the kitchen and toward the door. "This was really great of you. I know Mom will be, uh, thankful—uh, grateful. And happy." I picked up my boots. I could not get out of there fast enough. Holding my boots to my chest, I stepped onto the porch. My socks soaked up the dirty, melted snow.

I walked home in shame. Ashamed that I lied. Ashamed that we had no money. Ashamed that I manipulated them. Ashamed that I wished I'd done better than a twenty. Was I no better than my father? Or my mother? What was I going to say to George and Betty when I couldn't repay them?

Mom was waiting in the living room when I got home. Even though it was nearly three in the afternoon she was still wearing her nightgown.

"It took you long enough. Did you get any?"

I handed her the twenty-dollar bill and ran to the bathroom to wash my face. I felt filthy. I had to do something to get the shame off of me. But no matter how hard I scrubbed, the shame clung to me, absorbing into my every fiber.

. . . .

I carried that story of shame for well over twenty years. It shaped my reality about money, family, and relationships as it insidiously took control of my life.

Right now, you might be feeling the shame of your past. Perhaps my story triggered some of your old fears. While the details of our stories are different, what has brought us together on this journey is that we've allowed our stories to define us. We've subconsciously let these stories shape our realities. Just like zooming in on that beautiful sunset photo until all we see is sand, we can no longer see how big and beautiful our life is meant to be.

And that's not all our stories do.

HOW OUR STORIES LIMIT US

Imagine you've won a five-minute shopping spree at Costco. You're so excited! You think about everything you want—all the appliances, electronics, and jewelry. Then you locate where those items are in the store and the best route to get to each one. If your plan works, you'll get everything you want before the clock runs out. But then, on the day of the spree, you arrive to find out that the shopping spree is limited to the cleaning supply area of the store. Instead of running around excitedly throwing diamond rings and speaker systems into your cart, you mosey down the two designated aisles and end up with a case of toilet bowl cleaner and a jumbo pack of paper towels.

This is exactly what happens when we allow our stories to limit us. Instead of filling our lives with a true sense of self-worth, wild adventures, and meaningful connections before our clocks run out, we roam the same confined space and accept toilet bowl cleaner as a prize, believing that's all we're worthy of.

That's certainly what happened to me. After all my childhood trauma, I walked through my early adult life in an emotional silo yet still feeling vulnerable and exposed, certain that everyone could see my raw, gaping wounds. As a result, I felt less than. I closed myself off from life to protect myself from more harm. I made decisions based on fear. I said no—a lot. No to invitations. To adventures. To possibility. I worried incessantly about what people thought of me, which in turn reinforced my fawning, people-pleasing nature. I craved more but continually settled for less. Truth be told, though, my self-sabotaging inner banter wouldn't have let me accept more even if it were handed to me on a silver platter.

I was living a life of limitation.

Maybe you are, too?

If we're going to create a fuller life experience, we must become aware of how our stories limit us. Here are just a few ways our false tales damage our inner landscape.

WE OPERATE FROM SCARCITY INSTEAD OF ABUNDANCE

When we live inside our stories, we see the world from a place of scarcity and lack. For some of us that means we believe we're unworthy of love, happiness, and healthy relationships. Often this scarcity mindset is the result of not fully connecting with our caretakers early in life. It can also stem from doing without life's necessities, such as food, utilities, and shelter, as trauma around money can foster significant stories of limitation.

My earliest memories were of not having much—of living in a basement apartment and eating peanut butter and jelly out of the jars. A few years later, when Dad made better money, we moved into our ranch-style house on the nicer side of town. Mom bought me designer dresses, as they were the "uniform" of the private school I was now attending. When Dad went to prison a few years after that, my world upended. He'd installed a safe in the floor of the master bedroom closet and filled it with money. But long before he returned home, the only thing to be found in the safe was the gun he'd left for our "protection."

My mother didn't know how to budget the money and ensure our survival. Instead, she spent every penny buying designer clothes and lavish birthday cakes, even when it was no one's birthday. Her sense of unworthiness drove her shopping addiction. Spending money was her go-to way of soothing her anxiety. And when there was no more money to buy herself a "fix," she fell into complete despair.

With her erratic and irresponsible spending, my mother unknowingly wrote the plot for my money story. The pendulum swing of having little money to having an abundance of money to having none made me believe that money was illusory—that at any given moment, it, too, would abandon me just when I needed it most. As a result, I wrote a story about money and my value in the world based on scarcity.

The years I spent living in deprivation negatively affected my sense of worthiness. Even after earning my law degree and becoming a well-respected lawyer, I had trouble accepting that my work had monetary value. I never pressed for higher fees or a bigger raise. I settled for what the patriarchy told me I was worth.

When we consistently make choices from a place of scarcity, we send an energetic signal to the Universe that this is all we expect. If we want to break the cycle, we must believe we are worthy of abundance.

WE MAKE CHOICES BASED ON FEAR

Another way our stories limit us is with fear. They scare us into believing that the world is too big and we are too small. Many of us, rocked by limitation, let fear be our guide. We make small, safe choices instead of bold, courageous ones because no one ever taught us that it's okay to be bold.

Maybe we took the torch of fear from our parents or grandparents. Maybe we believed a small life was a safe life. That's certainly what I believed.

Terrified of being abandoned and perpetually unloved, I often made decisions out of fear. I chose friends, lovers, and jobs I didn't want because I was terrified of being left in the world alone. When I was twenty-four, I graduated from law school. A year later, I married Max. He was a stable guy who said he loved me. I'd like to say I was in love with him, but that wouldn't be completely true.

When I was with Max, my life, for the first time, felt solid and safe, mostly because he didn't require anything from me emotionally. In stark contrast to my parents, whose happiness I'd felt responsible for my entire life, Max didn't expect me to make him happy. I didn't have to worry about his emotional or financial well-being. I also felt secure with Max because his emotional distance kept our present life safe from my past. It was in this space where I stored my shameful memories of Mom and Dad. With Max I could emotionally cocoon inside myself without him noticing how deeply tucked away I was. My littleness was enough for him, and I found his aloofness comforting.

A byproduct of our emotional vacancy was our lack of intimacy. Even when my practiced love for him was at its pinnacle, ours was a flat, passionless love that left me scanning restaurants for a stranger who might light me up with desire. But my story convinced me that I couldn't trust love and intimacy, and that closed off with Max was where I belonged.

When I first met Max, I was twenty-one; he was five years older. I still lived with Mom and was a senior at the local college. I had chosen to stay close to home so I could help take care of my two brothers and sister. Money from my part-time job was family income, and that was the expectation.

Max was an entrepreneur who enjoyed simple things like eating pizza while watching *Star Trek: The Next Generation*. It was our mundane conversations about Captain Picard and the Klingons that intrigued me the most. I marveled that he could watch a TV show in complete and utter peace without anyone asking for more Ragu sauce splashed on their rigatoni.

About a week after we met, he invited me to his house. He said to bring a swimsuit and that we'd sit in his hot tub and talk. I expected we'd do more than just talk, so I dug out an old neon pink and green one-piece suit with a big black zipper that stretched from my collarbone to my pubic bone. While my swimsuit screamed the '80s, and it was currently the mid-90s, it seemed sexy enough for a hot tub date in the Midwest.

Max lived alone in a starkly modern house in the woods that was cold and drafty by its nature. It was appointed appropriately for its bones, but I was unsettled by its airy nonchalance. My energy had nothing to grasp, nothing to ground me into warmth.

After a few pleasantries in the foyer, Max said, "This way," as he climbed the staircase.

"Is your hot tub upstairs?" I asked, walking skeptically behind him.

"Well, it's not really a hot tub. It's more a bathtub . . . with jets."

"So we're going to sit in a bathtub . . . with our swimsuits on?" This was getting weirder by the second.

"It's great. You'll see." At the top of the staircase, he opened his bedroom door.

Something in me said to stop, and so I did, with five more steps to go. I didn't know what it was—the cold house in the woods, the faux hot tub, or this unfamiliar body coaxing me toward a bathtub . . . with jets, where I'd sit wearing a swimsuit—but it just didn't feel right. Something was missing. Ease? Warmth? Excitement? All of the above? But then again, what did I know about any of those things?

Max turned on his bedroom light and stretched his arms across the door frame. "You coming?"

Ignoring my intuition, I threw out some trust. He did seem harmless. And he was successful and cute. And he was closer to my age than any other guy I'd dated; I had a thing for older guys. Maybe I could give his faux hot tub a chance?

Within a few awkward minutes, we were sitting in the bathtub . . . wearing our swimsuits. Over the roar of the jets, he told me about his parents and that he wasn't really Jewish. Well, he was, but the family didn't practice. His mom had converted to Judaism before she married his dad, and that was the most Jewish thing that had happened to them. *So he's a faux Jew with a faux hot tub? What am I supposed to make of this?*

As the water grew tepid, so did my mood. I was completely confused. What was I doing here? He seemed interested in me, but there was no move in my direction. He stayed on his side of the tub the entire time as if there were a wall between us. *Maybe he wanted to be friends? Who bathed together? In swimsuits?* As strange as this all was, I stayed in Max's faux hot tub. He was smart and successful, and most importantly, he liked me. What was so wrong with that? Goosebumps spread over my cold body. I shivered.

Max touched my leg and leaned in for a kiss. I didn't feel a thing. Not a zing up top or butterflies down below. I chalked it up to high expectations since his lips were so full and juicy. It wasn't fair to put that much pressure on a kiss, was it?

A few minutes later, wrapped in a faded beach towel, I stood at the foot of his bed. He tossed me a pair of boxer shorts and a T-shirt without so much as a glance my way and flicked on the TV.

"Do you want to sleep over?"

I'd slept at a man's house more than a few times before and was never asked to put clothes *on*.

"Um, sure. Should I wear these?" I held the folded stack toward him.

"Unless you want something warmer, sweatpants or something?"

This was mind-boggling. He didn't seem attracted to me, and I wasn't attracted to him. What were we doing? Having a friendly sleepover, even though we weren't friends? As odd as it was, I agreed to stay because sleeping with a near-stranger in a cold house while wearing a faded Budweiser T-shirt was better than going back home to my mother and the wet blanket of responsibilities I could never elude.

In bed, we lay next to each other, not touching, while the flickering TV lit up our faces. He laughed right on cue at the sitcom's laugh track while I stared at him out of the corner of my eye. *Was he going to talk to me? Say anything at all? Should I say something?* When I couldn't handle the awkwardness any longer, I asked, "Are you sure I should stay?"

"Sure. It's fine. I have an early meeting but stay."

I didn't know what to do. Hug him? Kiss him? Roll over and ignore him? I stretched my leg out until my foot met his. He clicked off the TV.

"Turn over," he said. "I'll spoon you."

I did, and he did. We slept like that until morning.

And still, I felt nothing.

Because of my fear, I wrote a story that I was unworthy of love, joy, and desire. As a result, I stayed safe and passionless with Max until the pain of it all became too much to bear. I didn't overcome this particular story for several years. (More on this juicy topic later!) It was only when I became aware of how my story limited me that everything shifted.

What is fear anyway? Some have succinctly defined it by the acronym False Evidence Appearing Real. In all its irrational forms, fear is a defense mechanism created by our brains to keep us safe. And so we plod along, allowing fear to limit our lives. We do the "right" thing. We make safe decisions. Or worse yet, we make no decision at all because we're scared.

But I'm here to tell you that if you let it, fear will keep you from love. It will cheat you of greatness. It will close you off from the world. Fear is what holds us back from who we're meant to be, which is nothing less than a magnificent creature of the Universe who deserves to live a limitless life.

OUR STORIES LEAVE US LANGUISHING

Another way our stories limit us is that they leave us languishing. Old stories of abandonment and trauma will require us to settle. They'll insist we seek shelter. We may crave more from life—more passion, more pleasure, more joy—but we'll routinely accept less. In turn, we settle for a half-life, one that's neither fully present nor awake. We shuffle through our days, task-oriented, not joy-oriented. And many of us will crest on waves of apathy that will periodically break hard and fast on the shores of depression.

That was certainly my experience. I spent my first few years practicing law wishing I was doing anything but. I went to law school as a ticket out of poverty. I knew I had to have a steady career to support Brandon, my nine-year-old brother, whom I'd adopted after Mom died. I suppose I was also subconsciously trying to save my dad and the twelve-year-old me he left behind. I knew it was impossible to go back in time and rescue us from poverty and shame, but the lawyer in me wished I could. I often wondered, *How would my life have been different had Dad not gone to prison? Would I have had a childhood? Would I have married Max?* Those unanswerable, rearview mirror questions plagued me for years as

I trudged from courtroom to courtroom defending clients. But no matter the victory, nothing in my body resonated above *meh*. Life was flatline until depression roared in fast and hard for the first time a year into practicing law. It laid all its weight on me, disabling my gumption to even roll out of bed.

How about you? Are you settling? Are you lying in bed depressed? Are you afraid to get out from under the covers and face the life that awaits you? Do you find the bedsheet grazing your body equally comforting yet scratching your skin in such definitive motion that it may scrape away your being? Languishing is a form of non-existence that will swallow you whole and make you falsely believe that its colorless confinement is exactly where you're supposed to be. I'm here to tell you that you have the power (and the freedom!) to choose. You can lie under that scratchy sheet languishing and afraid of life, or you can wear it like a cape and crusade your way to a joyous life. I chose the latter.

And you can, too.

OUR STORIES LEAVE US IN CONSTANT FIGHT OR FLIGHT

After I divorced Max, I bought a tiny house in a coastal Florida town and lived alone for the first time in my life. Before marrying him, I'd spent nearly every conscious moment in tune only to the emotional and physical needs of my mother, brothers, and sister, while completely ignoring my own. When I finally broke free from everyone, I didn't know who I was, what I needed, or how to soothe my inner turmoil.

The busy days at work and lazy weekend afternoons reading in the sun were bearable. But the lonely nights terrorized me. Without the distraction of my loveless marriage, I was left with nothing standing between my past and me. Nightly, I was plagued by panicked dreams.

Me as a child. My parents. The hair pulling. The bloody lips. Hiding with my sweet puppy Whoopsie under the covers. I'd awake drenched in sweat, short of breath, unable to fall back to sleep. My heart racing, I'd leap out of bed and pace the floor, trying unsuccessfully to calm myself.

As terrifying as that time was, I'd spent decades living in fight or flight, so the feeling of panic was common to me. Sometimes my middle-of-the-night hysteria made it crystal clear that I was in full fight-or-flight mode. But it was the years of milder panic and anxiety, the daytime malaise, and general restlessness that made me sense that my body was still in survival mode.

And it was my stories of the past that shackled me there.

As we learned earlier, when we suffer repeated trauma in childhood, our emotional brain tries to protect us with fight, flight, or freeze. With enough time and continued chaos, our nervous system becomes dysregulated and gets stuck in overdrive. Add to it that when we constantly relive our old stories of trauma, our body stops knowing the difference between the past and the present. It feels our negative emotional energy and stays engaged to "protect" us by pumping a cocktail of stress hormones, like adrenaline and cortisol, through our bodies. Existing in this limited physical realm of fight or flight is a byproduct of living our old stories. We must be willing to let go of the story if we want a peaceful, joy-filled body and a limitless life.

OUR STORIES PLAGUE US WITH SELF-SABOTAGING BELIEFS

Our stories also limit us by filling our heads with untrue nonsense. You know what I'm talking about, all the self-sabotaging lingo that sounds like this:

I'm not enough.

I'm not smart, or brave, or adventurous.

I stink at relationships.

I'm not worthy of love or money or a fulfilling life.

Sound familiar? I know. Me too. These tragic words wield gargantuan power over us, and they often cause us to do less, try less, and be less, which in turn, makes it difficult to stop the cycle. These self-sabotaging cruelties are the subtext to our stories. And while we may not say these things about ourselves to others, our actions or, even more so, our inaction tells those in our sphere exactly how we feel about ourselves and what we think we're worthy of. If you're ready to change your inner dialogue, stay tuned. I'll teach you how to change your self-talk to a default of love and respect later in the book.

LET'S SUM IT UP

Learning how our story has shaped our reality and limited our life is crucial to understanding how powerful our stories are. Armed with this knowledge, we'll see where we've been and that our stories have not served us. Reeling in our trauma-induced stories, our reality becomes a cropped version of life. Not only are beauty and joy no longer on the horizon, they aren't even in the picture. From that distorted perspective, our stories limit our lives when they:

- make us believe in scarcity instead of abundance
- cause us to make decisions based on fear
- keep us languishing—we want more but accept less
- leave us in fight-or-flight overdrive
- fill our minds with sabotaging self-talk

. . . .

NOW IT'S YOUR TURN

Here's where we uncover how your stories have shaped your reality and limited your life. Grab your journal. Turn off your phone. Get cozy. Close your eyes and take a few deep breaths. Ask for clarity and relax into your heart space. There are no wrong answers to these questions. This is your opportunity to see how your stories are limiting you from being a fully alive, vibrant crusader of love and joy.

Do you feel constrained in your life? How?

Does everyday life make you feel listless or anxious?

Do you say no often—to opportunities, to adventures, to relationships?

Do you shy away from new experiences?

Share three examples of when and why you've said no to opportunities.

What are you most afraid of? Being alone? Being abandoned? Being judged? Disliked? Rejected? Failing? Succeeding?

What decisions have you made based on that fear?

How have your limiting beliefs affected your choices about . . .
   Education?

   Your career?

   Money?

   Your relationships with friends, lovers, and family?

Do you shy away from intimacy? Are you afraid of being hurt?

Are you afraid people won't like the real you? Why?

What dream are you not chasing because you feel limited or like you can't?

Do you say mean things to yourself?

Such as?

What does that stem from?

Have you ever found yourself sacrificing joy because you felt you weren't deserving? Give an example.

How has your money story been dictated by family trauma?

When you look at your life, do you see abundance or scarcity?

Are you settling? Are you afraid of going after what you want most?

What's something you want to achieve but don't feel capable or worthy of?

Do you crave more? More love, joy, success, adventure, freedom, sex, laughter, or abundance? Do you feel worthy of these things?

Please honor what you shared in these answers and know that these limiting words and beliefs are not you. They are the byproduct of the stories you adopted. There is no shame in what you uncovered. There is only love and the understanding that the way out of these limiting stories is through. Through the muck. Through the deception. Through the past.

To make sure we end this exercise full of abundance, I'd like you to write down three beautiful things about yourself and your life and one thing you most desire.

Now close your eyes and visualize that thing you most desire right in front of you. Wrap your energy around it and feel its warmth. Smile and welcome it into your life. When you're ready, take three deep breaths and give yourself some love.

You deserve love and abundance, not the stories that limit you with their fear, scarcity, and cruel subtext. No matter what you uncovered here, know that I've been there, too, and trust that I'm here with you now.

If you're ready, let's keep going.

5

· · · · · · ·

WHO WOULD YOU BE WITHOUT YOUR STORY? SHEDDING THE VICTIM MINDSET

C an you imagine how different your life could be if you didn't filter every bit of it through the false story your emotional brain created? What if, instead, you filtered your life through a lens of gratitude? That mindset shift can be difficult, especially when our story makes it nearly impossible for us to see the good we have in our life, let alone be grateful for it. So often we get caught up in the misery of the past, even when the circumstances of our present life may be worth more gratitude than we recognize. Instead, we feel victimized by our past traumas, and we allow the painful narrative we've written about them to cloud our perspective.

Why do we allow our trauma and the story we create about it to define our happiness? Because we've been conditioned. Our stories make us feel safe, subconsciously at least. That seems strange, right? But do they ever! We live with them for so long that they become ingrained in us. We mentally, emotionally, and spiritually exist on autopilot, navigating the sea of life with robotic responses. In turn, our pain points are triggered again and again.

And in that dysfunctional state of being, in that view of life through a tiny porthole, we can feel strangely secure. Our relationships repeat the same patterns. Our happiness level blips only a decibel or two above *meh*. We say no even before we're asked a question. As a result, some of us have donned a cloak of victimhood so heavy it keeps us from engaging with the world in an authentic and meaningful way.

But what if we could stop victimizing ourselves? Shift out of autopilot? Break our conditioning? Who would we be without our story?

I had many stories of shame and unworthiness that were rooted in my childhood. But my woe-is-me story about being a felon's daughter stuck especially hard, shaping my professional life as a young lawyer. It never occurred to me that my life could be different because I'd planted myself so deeply in the idea that I was, and always would be, a felon's daughter. That self-victimization imprisoned me until a wise mentor helped me see things differently.

. . . .

I'd hoped that being a smart, tough, ethical lawyer would rid me of the shame I felt about Dad. But in my gossipy, close-knit town, everyone knew he went to the clink. So no matter how hard I tried or how good I was, I'd drift off to sleep knowing that regardless of how many clients I saved, I couldn't go back in time and save Dad from prison—that was too long ago, too far away.

I often thought about the day when my world, as dysfunctional as it was, got even crazier. I was about eleven. Dad was mowing the front lawn. I'd stepped outside to fetch the mail, when the same man who I'd noticed sitting outside our house on and off for weeks drove up again. He parked on the street and turned off the engine. Dad stopped the mower and beckoned me closer. I stood motionless on the front porch. Dad waved at me incessantly until I met him in the grass. As we walked across the front yard toward the beige sedan, I prayed that Dad knew what he was doing.

We stood next to the driver-side window, allowing me to see the man behind the wheel up close for the first time. His slicked-down hair, parted on the side, emphasized his large square-frame glasses. There was an open notepad on his lap. The metal spiral across the top held a BIC pen.

He looked straight ahead as if we weren't there. The hair on my arms stood on end.

"Looks like this guy's gonna be sittin' outside our house every fuckin' day, so when you see him, just wave and say hi. Like this, see?" Dad waved dramatically and smirked.

"Uh huh," I said, tugging on Dad's other hand. I was terrified that the man was going to get out of his car, punch Dad, and kidnap me.

The man stayed put but took the pen from his notebook and scribbled some notes. Illegible as they were, I knew he was writing about us.

"That's right, sit there like a coward and write your bullshit notes. Nothin' to write about here, buddy," Dad said.

My heart pounded through my ears. "Dad, please. Let's go." I tugged his hand until he relented and walked with me back into the yard.

The next few steps were a blur of green and Dad's muffled profanity. When we got inside, Dad latched the deadbolt on the front door. I sobbed as fear and relief flooded my body in equal measure. Mom reached for me, but I tucked in tightly behind Dad.

He took my hand and led me to the kitchen. "Sit down. I need to tell you about the car lot."

Mom bit her thumbnail nervously. I sat down and dabbed my eyes with the hem of my T-shirt. "Who's the guy in the car, Dad?"

"Remember when I used to take you to the auction—"

"Who's the guy, Dad? Who is he?" I was yelling now, my face growing hotter with every syllable. In my eleven years, I'd never yelled at Dad before. Not even after all the nights he was gone and came back with his clothes smelling of other women's perfume. Not after all the times he beat Mom and never said he was sorry. But the omnipresent man camped out in front of our house terrified me like nothing had before.

"He's an FBI agent. And he thinks I did something wrong."

"Is he a police officer?"

"Yes, for the federal government."

I glanced at Mom, who was leaning against the stove crying.

"Are you going to jail?" I asked.

"No, no, no. I'm not going anywhere. I promise. I didn't do anything wrong. Let me explain it to you." He reached for a pad of paper and a pencil.

Over the next half hour Dad explained how he mastered the wrecked car business. He bragged about the perfect bodywork he did, which enabled him to make lots of money. He also explained that the FBI thought he was rolling back odometers and falsifying titles. Selling cars with altered mileage and not disclosing that the cars had been wrecked was, in the federal government's opinion, how Dad made his money, and all of it was illegal.

My anger subsided as I nestled lovingly into Dad's lengthy explanation. It was like the old days when he taught me how to count money and showed me how to spread Bondo on wrecked quarter panels. He wanted me to understand how he made money, and he thought I was smart enough to get it. I hadn't felt that connected to him in years, and in that moment, I bought his story like any naïve customer wanting a used Plymouth.

"So, you see, it's not illegal." He circled a section of his diagram and drew an arrow back to another part as he emphasized, "Nothing about what I'm doing is illegal."

Mom had begun making Hamburger Helper, but when Dad professed his innocence, she stood with her hands on his shoulders, nodding in silent agreement. In that skewed microcosm, the three of us could have been a real family. And for a few moments, I sat there, basking in our fleeting unity. But then logic smacked me across the face, catapulting me back to reality.

"But wait—if what you're doing isn't illegal, then why is a police officer sitting in front of our house watching everything we do?" I asked.

"Well, even if it is illegal," Dad puffed on his Black & Mild, "they can't prove it."

I slid my chair back and buried my face in my hands. I waited until my tears splattered on my legs before I looked back up at him. I wouldn't give him the satisfaction of seeing me cry—ever again.

I ripped up his diagram and threw it at him. "I hate you. For this and for everything you've done."

My disgust for him in that moment was not because I was surprised by his quasi-confession. I'd come to learn that, in dealing with Dad, there were as many sides to a story as he needed there to be. When he came home with lipstick on his collar, his first defense was there wasn't lipstick on his collar. This was known as the "who you gonna believe, me or your lying eyes" defense. Alternatively, if he admitted there was lipstick on his collar, he had no idea how it got there. This was known as the "I had nothing to do with it" defense.

Years later I realized that Dad, who was the master of loopholes, was training me to think hard and fast like a defense lawyer—or a criminal. But at that time, my heart was still beating like a girl betrayed by her father. I'd continued to love him even when he stopped taking me to work with him in the summer and made me stay home with Mom. I loved him when he stopped saying he was proud of me. I even loved him when he'd leave us for days and sleep with other women.

But that day in the kitchen, I realized that Dad hadn't made his half-hearted confession to me because he was sorry. He made it because he got caught, or because like any compulsive liar worth their salt, he believed his own bullshit. And realizing that your dad is running you like any other game is enough to break your heart wide open.

Years later, even though part of me was still that eleven-year-old girl victimized by being a felon's daughter, I knew I had to consider who I'd be without that story. If I stayed a victim, if I let the story I wrote about my father going to prison fuel me, I knew my chances of not only thriving but surviving were nil. Others in my town who had similar stories turned to alcohol or drugs or became felons themselves. Education had to be my drug of choice if I was going to survive. And so I went to law school.

But it wasn't long after I started practicing law that my story about being a felon's daughter came roaring back when a judge asked if my father was the criminal who rolled back odometers in the '80s. Part of me couldn't believe he was so bold, while the other part of me felt I deserved his inquisition. My imposter syndrome was operating at full tilt, and I expected I'd be "found out" sooner rather than later.

As a well-educated lawyer, I fought hard, trying desperately to be something other than a shame-filled girl whose dad served time in a federal penitentiary. But there weren't enough degrees, accolades, or external validation to heal my gaping emotional wounds. Luckily, I had a wise mentor who reminded me that the crimes of the father are not the crimes of the daughter. And, if I continued on like this, I would emotionally and mentally imprison myself for the rest of my life. Then she said something that upended my story.

"If you want to stop hurting, stop playing the victim."

STOP PLAYING THE VICTIM

For those of us who have suffered abuse and violence, we are indeed the victim of the event and the person who inflicted the trauma upon us. However, that does not mean we are destined to be the victim forever. It means that in that limited situation, there was a perpetrator and a victim. As the victim, we get to decide what we do with the aftermath of the trauma. If we allow the emotional brain to concoct a tale that makes us feel dirty, ashamed, unworthy, or less than, we will give our power to the perpetrator and live in victimhood.

If we, instead, choose to disavow the sad story and stand in our power, we can shed the victim mindset. The trauma, the origin of your story, is not who you really are. It is not who you are here to be. We are so much more than the sad, unfortunate things that happen to us. If we want to find ultimate emotional freedom, we must stop imprisoning ourselves in victimhood.

Here are the three things we must believe if we are to shed the victim mindset.

THE TRAUMA DIDN'T HAPPEN BECAUSE WE DESERVED IT

Often, the traumas that impact us most significantly aren't due to anything we've done or set into motion. A skewed sense of perfectionism can often lead us right into this false narrative. For example, we might think: *If I would have said this or done that, or if I were better or smarter or kinder, this wouldn't have happened to me.*

I witnessed this storyline in my law practice repeatedly. Some of my clients, who were charged with serious crimes, had their own traumas and resulting stories that set their lives on an altered course. Some were raped, abused, or abandoned. Some lived in extreme cyclical poverty. Yet, they victimized themselves and carried the weight of self-blame even though none of the trauma they experienced was their doing. Deep down they wanted more from life. Instead, they wrote a story of their unworthiness that left them physically, emotionally, and spiritually imprisoned.

I, too, had this victimized mindset. For decades, I believed that if I were perfect or better or smarter, I could have saved my parents and maybe even my childhood. Because I drafted this intricate story of failure that ran incessantly in my mind, it took me years of healing to finally understand that in this lifetime I could never have done enough to change the course of my early life. It also took me decades to accept that none of what I tried to fix was ever my responsibility in the first place.

After years of victimizing myself and after visiting countless jails and prisons over the course of my career, I can tell you there's little psychological difference between physical lockup and imprisoning ourselves in victimhood.

YOUR STORY IS A DISTORTION

To shed the victim mindset, we must remember that our story is a distortion created by the emotional brain to create "safety" around the trauma. Sadly, there's no safety in our false tales of fear, loss, scarcity, sadness, betrayal, and blame. And of course, let's not forget blame's overbearing sister, shame. Remember: the story we write is the emotional interpretation of the event and not the facts of the event itself.

To better understand, let's pretend you're testifying in court about being robbed. You're asked to tell the jury what happened when the perpetrator approached you. You reply, "I have trouble trusting strangers and can't go out alone anymore. I can't help but wonder what I did to deserve this. I shouldn't have been walking alone, wearing my nice watch. If only I'd been smarter about it all, I wouldn't be in this situation. It's all my fault."

The opposing counsel rightfully objects, and the judge directs you to only testify to the facts of what happened: Where were you? What time was it? Did you see the person's face? What were they wearing? What did they say? Did they have a weapon?

This difference is between the facts of what you experienced (your trauma) and your emotional brain's interpretation of what happened (your story). For most of us, the story is where we get caught up. It's crucial that we see our story as nothing more than an emotional distortion of our trauma and who we think we are because of it.

THERE'S A BIGGER PURPOSE

The third step in shedding the victim mindset is to find the bigger purpose in your trauma—a deeper meaning for what happened. This can undoubtedly be challenging, especially when we're talking about abuse and violence. However, I can tell you that out of my own trauma of emotional and physical abuse, I found a bigger purpose for it all than just the pain.

I am not saying there is a greater purpose for suffering, but I am saying that if we dig deeper, we might find a ray of light that wasn't there before. What I've discovered, what I strive for now after rising above my story, is a greater sense of gentleness, empathy, and compassion for myself because of what I went through. I also relish who I am, what I will endure, and what I will never sign up for. I know how to honor myself and others, how to stand with them when they need me, and how to let them experience consequences when theirs is not my battle to wage. I have clear and definitive boundaries that keep me true to who I am. No longer sacrificing my own happiness for others, I've given up people pleasing. Instead of slogging through life, I move with focused purpose and brilliant intention. And guess what happens when you practice shining your own light on the world? People are drawn to you and want to emulate your energy. This means that just by being YOU, you are helping people.

One of the biggest gifts we can unearth from our trauma is gratitude. Feeling grateful was a powerful catalyst in my healing. Every day, multiple times a day, I feel gratitude for who I am because of what I lived through. Notice that I said I *feel* gratitude. I don't espouse the clichéd version of gratitude that's as ubiquitous as the reclaimed wood signs touting thankfulness sold at HomeGoods. No. I don't just say I'm thankful. I've taught myself how to change my emotional resonance to one of radiant gratitude for every aspect of my life. I cry tears of joy that I've come out the other side of my traumas (and the stories I wrote about them) not only intact but keenly aware of my abundance. Stay tuned—I'll share my tried-and-true gratitude practice in more detail later in the book.

I've also uncovered the silver linings in my traumas. My most beloved friends are those who've risen above their stories and are brave enough to share them with me. We talk freely about our traumas and the stories we created because of them. We cheer for each other when we reach our next level of emotional, spiritual, and professional rising. Also, because of my trauma, I've moved geographically to places that feed my soul, connected with people who've lifted me up, and tapped into a treasure trove of resilience that fuels my every step.

What gifts can you unearth in your trauma?

LET'S SUM IT UP

Victimhood is the byproduct of the false stories we write after enduring trauma. Often, our victimhood becomes so ingrained that we can't see how beautiful our current lives are. To shed the victim mindset, we must:

- accept that the trauma didn't happen because we deserved it
- understand that our stories are distortions created by the emotional brain
- create a bigger purpose for our trauma

Once we shed the victim mindset, we can feel the abundance in our lives.

. . . .

NOW IT'S YOUR TURN

Who could you be if you stopped victimizing yourself and stood in your own power? Who could you be if your story were different? Perhaps someone filled with joy? Someone who laughs and lives in the present instead of the past? Could you create a bespoke life of wonder, adventure, and abundance? You certainly can. And that is what awaits you once you shed the victim mindset.

Now, grab your journal and dive into these questions. There's a part of you that's waiting to be heard—the part of you that wants to stop playing the victim. Likely, there's more than one hurt or trauma that's holding you back, and that's completely normal. Answer the following prompts as many times as needed to release the stories that are imprisoning you as a victim.

What was the original hurt or trauma? Be as factual and objective here as possible. (If needed, refer to your answers to the prompts in chapter 3.)

What about this situation made you feel victimized? Because this happened, you felt . . .

Has feeling like a victim made life feel easier or harder for you?

Do you feel weak or empowered carrying around those old, victimized feelings?

In your wildest dreams, what does a life of abundance look like?

How might your victim mindset be keeping you from that life?

Can you see the situation from another perspective? What does that look like? (This is not about forgiving other people [yet!], but it is about looking at the situation through an objective lens.)

List one positive that came from the situation. I know this may be challenging, but I'm asking you to dig deep here. Can you find a silver lining? (Someone you met. Something you learned. A place you moved to. A career you chose.)

I know this was tough, and you might even want to quit. But don't. Change like this is never easy for anyone. That resistance to change you may feel is your emotional brain coaxing you into the autopilot existence you've grown accustomed to. Subconsciously, we strive to maintain equilibrium. Our emotional brain likes routine and doesn't want us expending energy by changing our thought patterns. It's like when that little voice tells you to stop exercising because your legs are burning. Your brain will want to default to its old pattern if an idea feels challenging or uncomfortable.

Trust that I'm here with you and all your messy glory. I honor your courageous spirit. I want you to honor yourself, too. This is difficult work, but you are uncovering who you could be without that old, limiting story. I hope you feel the beauty and promise of what is to come. You are exactly where you need to be as we venture into the next phase of our healing adventure—releasing the story.

Part 2

. . . .

RELEASING THE STORY

As I walked out the door toward the gate that would
lead to my freedom, I knew if I didn't leave my bitterness
and hatred behind, I'd still be in prison.
—Nelson Mandela

6

. . . .

HOW DID YOU GET TANGLED UP IN YOUR STORY?

B y now you've acknowledged your story (high five!) and have a strong sense of how that story has limited your life. You're even saying sayonara to victimhood, your story's wretched byproduct.

But if you're like me, you don't have just one story, you have multiple. If you do, don't fret. It's perfectly okay to have more than one story. In fact, it's the norm. Most of us have multiple stories stemming from various traumas. And while each trauma yields its own narrative and limits our lives in all the ways we discussed previously, there's a tipping point when we become tangled up in our stories. It's when we first see that the canvas of our life is not just dotted with a few sad, untrue stories.

Rather, it consists *only* of our stories. Once we're entangled, we come to expect the worst for ourselves.

Entanglement can occur in several ways, including:

- enduring repetitive or long-term trauma
- our lineage—the multigenerational transfer of trauma
- how we were parented
- experiencing substantive setbacks
- unknowingly manifesting negative outcomes

Recognizing how we got tangled up in our stories is a powerful tool. As we learned earlier, we must become self-aware if we want to heal. With this awareness of how we got entangled, we can free ourselves from our current storied situation and ensure that we don't get tangled up in future stories.

To help you better understand how entanglement works, let's talk about latch hooking. I know this may feel like a sharp left turn but hear me out. Latch hooking was popular when I grew up in the eighties. (At least it was in Ohio, where cow tipping was also all the rage, but don't hold that against us.) If you're unfamiliar, latch hooking can be equated to knitting or crocheting. A latch hook kit contains a color-coded mesh canvas, hundreds of pieces of yarn of various colors and lengths, and a hook-like tool that's used to latch the yarns to the canvas.

Starting out, it's difficult to see how the individual pieces of yarn relate to the bigger picture. But after a while, and with enough repetition and hooking the yarns to the canvas, you don't see the individual yarns anymore. You only perceive the overall design—the visual story of the canvas.

Entanglement is much like this. With each disappointment, loss, and heartache, our stories about them become latched onto our emotional canvas. These stories are intricate, tightly woven yarns of untruths, each with their own length and intensity of color. With enough time and enough latching onto our mental landscape, our stories no longer feel like one-offs. Instead, we perceive them in total, as the landscape, the canvas, of our lives—as if our lives are made up of nothing *but* our stories. This is how we get tangled up in our stories, and it's certainly how I got tangled up in mine.

My mother and I experienced parent-child role reversal (also known as parentification) from as early as I can remember. I got tangled up in my story—that I wasn't worthy of much, including a childhood—day by day, bit by bit, yarn by yarn. With every meal I cooked for myself. Each time I filled the tub with the water I heated on our gas stove so my siblings could take at least a tepid bath. When I bought our food with lint-covered change and later with food stamps. While I'm not sure of the exact moment our roles officially reversed, one particular morning when I was about eight years old flickers the brightest.

. . . .

The house was oddly quiet and didn't smell like coffee as it normally did. I walked down the hall to Mom and Dad's bedroom and cracked open the door. Mom was curled up in the fetal position sobbing. Dad's side of the bed was smooth, the covers tucked in tightly around the mattress.

"Mom, where's Dad?"

"Just get ready for school," she said.

I went to the bathroom and brushed my teeth. Just as I finished, Dad came through the front door singing "Take This Job and Shove It." I met him in the kitchen. He was wearing the same polyester button-down he'd worn the night before. My stomach grew queasy.

"Dad, are you still taking me to school?"

"Sure, kiddo. Go get ready."

Mom walked in, her face blotchy and streaked with dried mascara. My feet stayed planted, but my anxiety climbed the walls. Without saying a word, Mom walked across the kitchen, opened the cupboard, and threw a plate at Dad's head. He ducked. Then he laughed. The sun shone brightly through the orange-and-yellow café curtains above the sink, casting an eerie aura around him.

"You stupid, ungrateful bitch! If nothing I do is enough for you, then let's just break it all!"

And one by one, Dad broke every dish we owned. Then he lunged at Mom, grabbed her by the throat, and dragged her to the floor by the sink. Mom's face turned as white as cotton as she clawed desperately at his hands. Her legs flailed. She kicked through the cabinet under the sink, knocking over bottles of cleaner. Sudsy liquids spilled and splashed on the floor.

I grabbed Dad's fingers and tried with all my might to pry them from Mom's throat. They felt like steel. I threw my arms around his neck and yelled in his ear, "Let go! Let go! You're killing her!"

As if I'd pushed a magic button, he released his grip. He stared at me wide-eyed for a moment before walking calmly out the front door. Mom rolled back and forth on the floor, gasping for life. Then she squeezed my hand as if she were dangling from a cliff.

"Breathe, Mom. Breathe." I said, wiping the tears from her cheeks. Her mouth moved, but no sound came out. I put my ear to her lips.

"I'm pregnant," she whispered.

I didn't know where babies came from. It seems my old soul knew how to stop a murder, but my young brain didn't yet know the laws of reproduction. I brushed her hair from her forehead. When her breath regulated, I helped her stand up. She stumbled toward her bedroom, brushing the wall with her shoulder the entire length of the hallway. Scared that Dad would come back and finish the deed, I locked the front door and pushed two kitchen chairs in front of it. For the first time, but certainly not the last, I felt responsible for my mother's survival.

Mom came out of the bedroom a while later wearing her Gloria Vanderbilt jeans, a white billowy top, and a scarf that hid Dad's fingerprints behind its pink, flower-printed silk.

"Let's go out." Her voice cracked.

I skipped school that day. We rode around in the convertible, the sun hot on our faces. We didn't listen to eight-track tapes like usual. We just listened to the wind—its hum filled with a freedom my mother would never experience in her lifetime.

While our role reversal continued over time, my story of being my mother's protector ensnared me four years later after Dad went to prison.

"Mom? Are you okay?" I stood in her bedroom doorway. She sat on the far side of the bed with her back against the nightstand. She had a gun in her hand—the gun Dad had left for our "protection."

Her voice, tinged with desperation, wavered strangely. "No, I'm not okay. We're out of money."

Dad hadn't even been gone a year. But in that short amount of time, she'd spent every cent he left us.

She didn't look anything like my mother. Her unwashed face was worn and wrinkled. She wore a green silk robe that I hadn't seen in years, the orange trim ragged and torn down the center of her naked breasts. Her toenails were long and ragged, her bare feet dirty and cracked. She shivered incessantly.

"Mom, here." I took the crocheted blanket from the bed and tried to cover her feet.

"Don't come any closer or I'll blow my fucking head off." She rested the muzzle of the revolver on her temple.

Terrified that she might kill us all, I pleaded, "Okay, okay, I won't. Please, Mom, don't do this. Put the gun down, please."

After minutes that felt like hours, I convinced her to hand me the gun.

My story—that I wasn't worthy of a childhood, fun, happiness, or much else for that matter—had already taken over my life. But when the woman who'd given birth to me, who was supposed to protect *me*, put a loaded gun in my small, trembling hands, I became so entangled in my story that I couldn't feel or see anything but the story I'd written to protect her.

HOW WE GET TANGLED UP IN OUR STORIES

Perhaps seeing how I got tangled up in my stories can shed some light on how you got tangled up in yours. Granted, how we get tangled up is often an intricate, tightly woven canvas of events, which makes it difficult to discern. However, if we want to heal, if we want to ultimately rise above our story, we must understand how we got tangled up in the first place. Cultivating this awareness is a crucial step in not only breaking free from our tangled mess of stories, but it also keeps us from getting tangled up in future stories.

Here are a few ways we can unknowingly get entangled in our stories.

REPETITIVE AND ONGOING TRAUMA

Experiencing repeated trauma is how we most readily get entangled in our stories. This can happen due to the ongoing nature of the abuse. For example, being parentified, as I was when I switched roles with my mother. It can also happen if the trauma is drawn out, long-lasting, or recurring. Maybe your parents had a lengthy, contentious divorce, or you had a parent or sibling who had a long illness, or perhaps you suffered from a debilitating injury.

The repetitive or drawn-out nature of the trauma mentally reinforces the false narrative that your emotional brain originally created while in survival mode. Each time the pain was inflicted or the longer the trauma lasted, the faulty circuitry of your emotional brain was strengthened, ensuring that your limiting story would eventually swallow you whole.

That was certainly my experience. My mother was undoubtedly a tortured soul who suffered from an undiagnosed mental health condition. This is not to excuse the role reversal she not only allowed but expected, but rather to offer perspective on the relentless nature of her abuse. After years of enduring her volatile behavior, I was tangled up in a story of worthlessness so thick, its viscosity bound me like quicksand. And so even as she approached death some twenty years later, I stayed at her side, unable to see anything other than the story that had defined every aspect of my being.

. . . .

Mom was emaciated and her face gaunt. Her bald head was spotted with patches of silver, making her appear decades older than her forty-four years. Her eyes glazed over, she fixed her line of sight out the window and onto the fiery fall leaves grasping their last bit of life.

"Those dying leaves are so pretty," she said while sitting on the portable toilet next to the bed. "Dying's not so pretty in here."

I diverted my eyes and floated a clean sheet over the mattress, causing Mom to shiver from its descending breeze. Her mood was just as chilly.

"So what if I wet the bed?" she snapped. "You know how many times I had to clean up your messes? This is the least you could do."

The air was thick and stunk of urine. I pulled the sheet taut and stifled the angry words percolating on my tongue, hoping my silence would diffuse her agitation. No such luck.

"I can't get out of bed on my own anymore. There, you happy? I said it. I'll be confined to that bed from here on out. Might as well just throw this toilet out the window"

"Then you'll wear diapers," I replied.

"I will never."

"Tell me, then. What do you think we should do?" I crossed my arms and leaned against the doorframe.

Her empty gaze bore through me.

With a tone of pleasurable authority in my voice, I said, "I'll tell you what I did do—I called hospice, and they're coming today."

"You did what? I told you I wasn't ready."

I straddled her legs, preparing to lift her back onto the bed.

"Don't touch me," she said.

"You getting in bed by yourself?"

She sat motionless.

"I didn't think so."

I laid her in bed, and she turned away from me, exposing a sore on her left butt cheek.

"What's this?" I touched the area around it. It was a pus-filled blister and had a foul odor.

"How should I know? You're the one taking care of me." She rolled over, blocking the sore from my view. "Just do something about it."

"I can't do this all by myself anymore. I can't take care of you and the kids and go to law school. I don't know how to make all this work. The doctor said hospice was a good idea, and I trust him."

"So because you're selfish, hospice has to come? Fine, but I'm not going anywhere."

"Whatever," I said, lifting her hips on top of a clean disposable pad.

She grabbed my face. "I'm not dying until I'm good and ready, you hear me?"

I flinched. Even though she hadn't beaten me in years, her bony fingers digging into my cheeks took me back to all the beatings and the countless nights she kept me awake until the sun rose, ranting about every awful thing that ever happened to her. Caring for her cancer-ravaged body despite her decades of abuse was the final yarn I hooked onto my storied canvas. It was the final tormented tale that entangled me.

OUR LINEAGE SETS THE STAGE

The multigenerational transfer of trauma is another way we get entangled in our stories. It occurs when one generation experiences trauma without the ability or opportunity to resolve it, which leads to the transference of that energy to the next generation.

When Mom was about six years old, her mother walked out on Mom and Mom's alcoholic father, who worked all day in the steel mill, until it was time to crack open a few beers after work. His mother, my great grandmother Stella, stepped in and cared for Mom. Stella was from Ukraine. After being abandoned by her own family when she was sixteen, Stella emigrated alone to the United States. She cared for Mom until she died of a heart attack when Mom was twelve. She was cold to the touch when Mom found her on the kitchen floor.

The unresolved trauma of loss and abandonment that my great-grandmother Stella experienced was passed on to her son, my mother's father, who later turned to alcohol to cope with the fact that his mother had been withdrawn and distant. His sense of worthlessness was then passed on to my mother, who was subsequently abandoned by every parent figure who was supposed to soothe and nurture her.

With time and distance, I can see why my mother disassociated herself from our family and didn't have the innate ability to mother anyone, let alone herself. I cannot condone her abusive and neglectful behavior, but I do see in my familial history a dysfunctional pattern woven into the fabric of our tenuous being. It was in our wiring—this expectation of abandonment and an inability to soothe ourselves, even as adults—that had generation after generation repeating stories of loss, shame, and worthlessness.

That being said, generational trauma does not sentence us to a lifetime of emotionally mutated DNA that forever entangles us in our untruthful stories. Quite the contrary. If we are to break free of these familial patterns, we must cultivate the awareness of our familial stories and how they can insidiously morph our life into darkness. We must vow not to succumb to them, but instead heal our trauma so we may ultimately rise above our story and end the generational transfer of our pain.

HOW WE WERE PARENTED

Even when our parents love us and have the best intentions, there are countless ways their actions, inactions, and words tonally reinforce our stories. Perhaps you had a parent who cared more about outward appearances or how the family looked to others than about how the family interacted behind closed doors. Maybe you grew up with a parent who expected you to follow in their professional footsteps or pushed you to achieve their unfulfilled dreams. While these parents want success and stability for their children, what they create instead is a limiting story that their children aren't capable of determining their own path and that they aren't worthy of the life they independently desire.

Or maybe you're like me and your mother was constantly consumed with her weight and body image. After years of cabbage soup dinners washed down with Diet Coke, I nearly drowned in the false stories about my body and the weight I didn't need to lose and could never shed.

Parents who seek validation from others (belonging to the *right* clubs, driving the *right* cars, and saying only the *right* thing) can also heave the undue burden of people-pleasing onto their children. When our parents impose their need for external validation on us, we don't develop the wherewithal to tune inward to our own desires. Instead, we might begrudgingly schlep to the club all summer and play tennis when, really, we want to go to creative writing camp or pitch a tent in the woods. These validation-seeking parents may also be successful professionals who expend most of their energy on clients, customers, or patients. This behavior stems from their own unresolved story of unworthiness as they strive for the acceptance and respect of society. Their devotion to their work leaves little time to show their children the love and devotion needed to cultivate their own sense of worth.

Do any of these parental patterns resonate with you? Seeing the parental patterns and tone that shaped your life is key to understanding how you got tangled up in your story.

EXPERIENCING SUBSTANTIVE SETBACKS

Setbacks such as a lost job or a divorce can jolt us into the harsh spotlight of perceived failure, ingraining a sense of worthlessness that reinforces our story. Early setbacks like losing awards, friendships, or team tryouts can cut deep and wound us just as much, if not more, than the setbacks that occur later in life.

That's certainly what happened to me at age eleven, when an honor I worked hard for was stripped from me when the school faculty found out that Dad was in trouble with the law.

. . . .

After months of surveilling our house, the FBI got a warrant for Dad's arrest. Perhaps Dad knew, which is why he left town a day before they showed up looking for him. When the feds realized Dad had skipped town, they splashed his photo across all the local TV channels, along with words like "wanted" and "at large."

Dad usually drove me to my Christian school on the other side of town, but since he was on the lam, Mom took me to school the next day. As I walked toward my sixth-grade classroom, students in the hallway buzzed about laughing and talking. I was relieved to be there with my friends and not stuck at home with Mom, who'd been a nervous wreck since Dad left, biting her fingernails to their bloody quick. But anxiety overcame me as I stood outside my classroom.

The students were seated and chatting loudly. When I got a few steps into the room, everyone stopped and looked at me. Had they seen Dad on TV? From her podium in front of the chalkboard, the teacher took note of my tentative stance and prodded me to sit down.

"Take your seat. Hurry, hurry. Let's get started," she said.

I slunk to my desk, diverting my gaze from the gaggle of my peers. I caught my friend Jaime's eye and half-smiled at her. She wrinkled her nose just like she did when her mom packed fruit instead of cookies in her lunch box. Did she know the police were looking for Dad? Afraid they all knew Dad was a fugitive, I slid down in the chair, my face burning with humiliation.

The teacher led us in prayer. Then, with excitement in her voice, she began the morning announcements. Between my buzzing, red-hot ears, this is what my eleven-year-old brain recorded.

"As you know, our class graduation is coming up. I've had a chance to look over all the test papers again, and we have a new list of top students for graduation," she said, shuffling papers on the podium.

Bewildered, I perked up. Just a few days before, the teacher had told me that I was going to be the valedictorian. What was this new list about?

She read the names off the list, and when mine wasn't first, my ears rang with an alarm of shame. I didn't hear my name called, but later, Jamie told me I was third.

When Mom picked me up that afternoon, I got in the car and slammed the door.

"What's wrong?"

"I'm not the valedictorian anymore," I said, angry tears filling my eyes.

"What? Why not?"

"I don't know. The teacher didn't say."

Mom threw the car in park right there in the middle of the pick-up line, got out, and slammed her door harder than I had slammed mine.

"Let's go." She stormed toward the school entrance.

People honked their car horns and drove around us, but Mom didn't care. She grabbed my hand and marched into the school, straight down the hallway, and into the principal's office. Standing there in front of Mr. Hardwick, she was shoeless, but wearing her favorite socks—Pepto pink fold-overs with big red hearts. With sunglasses pushing back her wild, wavy hair and her eyes aflame with anger, she resembled a lion (with an inexplicable sock fetish) ready to pounce.

"How is it that my daughter is no longer the valedictorian?" I couldn't help but think Mom's incredulous tone was more about her own ego than about championing my cause. But, because it wasn't often that she stood up for me, I scowled at Hardwick, crossed my arms, and tucked in behind her right hip.

Hardwick leaned back in his chair. His robust belly framed a tie clip adorned with a gold Jesus hanging on a cross. "Well, her teacher looked over the final exams *again*, and two other students scored higher than your daughter."

"Bullshit. I know exactly what this is about. Don't lie to me."

"I'm sorry for what your family is going through, but she *will not* be the valedictorian." He folded his hands matter-of-factly on the desk.

Right then, in Mr. Hardwick's office, my story of worthlessness was reinforced in a way it hadn't been before. This was about more than just being valedictorian. This was about losing something I'd worked hard for, something that meant I was smart and worthy of something good outside of my dysfunctional, abusive home. It was also the first time I lost friendships. I hadn't had many friends up until then. Mom's mood swings and her tumultuous relationship with Dad made it challenging to have playdates outside of school. But these kids, who I laughed and learned with in my sixth-grade class, were the closest thing I'd had to friends. To feel shunned by them because of something my father did—something that was completely out of my control—tragically reinforced the story I'd written about my unworthiness, shame, and what it meant to be the daughter of a criminal.

Maybe you've experienced substantial setbacks, too? Have you let a personal or professional disappointment reinforce your story? As strange as it sounds, we will subconsciously validate our stories by perceiving setbacks as proof of our unworthiness. This is our brain maintaining the status quo by keeping us "safe" and locked away from the world. It's easy to get tangled up in our story when we subconsciously see setbacks as failures. We begin to wonder why we should even try.

UNKNOWINGLY MANIFESTING NEGATIVE OUTCOMES

The law of attraction can also cause us to get tangled up in our story. This universal law of energy, in its simplest form, states that whatever energy you put into the world, you get back. This means your thoughts, words, and actions define what will come into your life. Positive begets positive. Negative begets negative.

It's easy to see then how we can get tangled up in our stories with all this energy matching going on, right? Let's say you're carrying a story of worthlessness around, and while you aren't screaming it from the mountaintop, you're exuding it from your every pore. I know you don't mean to (I never did either), but even when you don't consciously project your insecurities into the world, you subconsciously do exactly that.

What you believe about yourself is what you attract. If you believe that you're only worthy of one-night stands, jobs beneath your ability, or friends who degrade you, then that's what you'll get. Like attracts like. The Universe matches our energy and feeds back to us what we put into the world. Therefore, if we want a different life, we must change what we believe about ourselves. We must believe we are worthy of abundance, love, and joy.

And we do this by untangling ourselves from our stories.

LET'S SUM IT UP

Now that we've acknowledged our story (or more likely, our stories) and we see how they've limited us, it's time to hone in on that unfortunate tipping point when we become tangled up in our story. It's when we no longer see just a handful of traumas and stories dotting our landscape. Instead, we perceive our entire life to be a canvas of sorrow, limitation, and fear. Sadly, it's tragically easy to get tangled up in our stories.

If our trauma is ongoing or repetitive, we can get entangled. We might also feel the multigenerational transfer of traumatic energy tethering us to our story. Our parents might set the tone of entanglement with their actions, inactions, or expectations. Setbacks such as a lost job, illness, or divorce can wrap our stories even more tightly around us. Finally, the law of attraction can serve up matching energy to our stories of unworthiness, thus tightening the bonds of our stories even more. There are many ways in which we can get entangled in our story, but becoming aware of how we got caught up is the key to unraveling ourselves.

NOW IT'S YOUR TURN

As we begin this work of untangling our stories, all I ask is that you dig in and cultivate that awareness we talked about early on—that you shine a light on the different ways in which you got tangled up in the first place. There is no right or wrong answer, and you will likely find that there were many reasons you got entangled, and that's perfectly okay.

This is *your* healing journey, and it will unfold as it needs to, in its own way and in its own time. Be patient and trust that I'm here with you every step of the way. All you have to do is follow the prompts and write down what comes to mind. This kind of free-flow question and response is how we unlock the past and view it objectively for what it is—a map of where we've been. It will also tell you exactly where you need to go next.

Have you experienced repetitive or long-term trauma?

As a child, did you experience parentification, where you switched roles with a parent?

What was your mother's story? Your father's? Was there a limiting story that shaped the lives of your parents or grandparents?

How did their stories impact you?

Did your parental figures model joy, fulfillment, and love?

Did they set healthy boundaries for themselves?

Were your parents overly concerned about the opinions of others?

Did they obsess about their own physical appearance or make you feel insecure or shameful about your own?

Were you expected to do activities or take classes that you weren't passionate about because your parents insisted?

Did you experience a setback or perceived failure early in life that reinforced your story?

Was there a traumatic event later in life (e.g., an illness, death, or divorce) that wove the story more tightly around you?

Were there friends, lovers, or family members who validated your false story?

Have you spent the years since your trauma expecting the worst or being pessimistic?

Hopefully you see the circumstances that entangled you in your story and how much of this reinforcement was beyond your control. And now, with the awareness of how entanglement happens and how you got caught up in your stories, you can join me as we uncover how your story took over your life.

7

· · · · · · · ·

WHEN YOUR STORY
TAKES OVER YOUR LIFE

H is eyes were as dark as night. That should've been my sign to run in the other direction—the windows of his soul shut tight, forbidding the light to shine in or out. But instead, I ran straight toward this man with my arms (and legs!) wide open and my eyes wide shut. This wasn't my first dysfunctional relationship, but it was the one that shook me so ferociously that I didn't know if I'd survive its aftermath. When Jack and I broke up, I hit the proverbial bottom so hard that every already-fractured piece of me shattered. Every cell in my body wept. Every obsessive thought held my parents, my ex-lover, and all their abandonment in equal measure. This is when my story nearly killed me.

When a story takes over your life, you're unable to make decisions that serve you. Freedom of choice is thrown out the window. Instead, everything in your life is filtered through the dirty, mucky lens of your overpowering story. You're subconsciously and instinctively drawn to the very thing that shackles you to your story. Even if it's abuse or addiction—even if it's killing you bit by bit—your emotional brain will default to the storyline. Over and over, you'll gravitate toward whatever keeps you languishing in your story. You'll say you hate it. You'll tell everyone that you don't know why this keeps happening to you. But you'll keep going back for more—more pain, more abandonment, more misery. This is how your story takes over your life.

And it's exactly how it took over mine.

. . . .

I wasn't even divorced when I started having the most titillating sex of my life with Jack. I was separated and living alone with divorce papers filed, an ending that would surely be my happily ever after. It's not that Max was a bad guy. I mean, he was solid, and he didn't require much of me emotionally. Add to it that his parents were the Cleavers compared to the lying, cheating, violent people I called Mom and Dad. Our divorce was more about how emotionally vacant we'd both been and what a black hole our sex life had always been.

We were acquaintances who shared toothpaste and went to bed in pajamas. I tried to make it better. I even bought books on how to be a sex goddess. I read them diligently, plotting my every move in the bedroom. When that didn't work, we signed up for weekly therapy sessions. Every Thursday at noon, we'd show up and pay a fabulous, fifty-plus-year-old woman $150 to counsel passion into our marriage.

After a few sessions, and still feeling no passion with Max, I began an erotic email affair with Jack. He was a long-term bachelor, nearly twenty years older than me, who I met through work. The rumor was that he had a bevy of ex-girlfriends, each prettier and younger than the last. But there was a spark between us that could not be ignored, so I hit "reply" each and every time he sent me an arousing message.

Max found one of these sexually charged emails and brought it to our next therapy session. He waved it around like a vindictive older brother desperate to have me grounded. I wouldn't give him the satisfaction.

Before our therapist could even sit down, I blurted out, "I've been having an email affair with a guy I know. And . . . he wants to have sex with me."

She sat down and crossed her legs, her face emotionless, as if all I said was it's hot outside. Maybe emails detailing oral sex and other orgasmic delights were a regular thing around here?

"And how does that make you feel?" she asked.

I closed my eyes. "Sexy. And alive. I want passion, once and for all. I want to be . . . fucked! You know? Finally, just . . . fucked." Part of me couldn't believe the words that came out of my mouth, but the naughty grin on my face said otherwise.

"And Max, how does that make you feel?"

After a few long seconds, the silence grew uncomfortable. I glared at him. *Come on, give me something.*

"Well? How does that make you feel?" I asked.

He looked at the therapist and replied sheepishly, "I'm happy with the way things are."

And suddenly, all the shackles that bound me to him were magically unlocked. I didn't feel anything for him anymore. Not love. Not hate. I didn't want him to quit watching television all night, every night, or stop slurping his drinks, or look at me with lust. I wanted only one thing.

"I want a divorce."

"What? You're going to give up what we have for some guy who just wants to fuck you?"

"Abso-fucking-lutely."

In that moment, I accepted that Max preferred me small and closed off and that he'd never want me to be any different. After all, that's what he signed up for when we got married. I didn't know how to not be small and closed off, but this sexually charged, pleasure-driven energy brewing inside me made me feel like maybe I could be different. Maybe I could be someone who felt pleasure and desire. Maybe I had value and worth and someone could actually love me. And maybe I'd finally be rid of Max *and* the memories of my dysfunctional family and all the shame they'd heaved upon me.

I drove back to work completely aroused. I craved something more than I'd ever experienced before. Something more sexually adventurous. Something with more giddy up. Something more . . . emotionally disastrous. (And let me just set this down right here: be super careful what you wish for because, as we learned about the law of attraction, you just might get it.) While I was consciously craving sexual excitement and physical connection, subconsciously, my story was leading me right down the same emotionally unavailable path I'd been down with Max. But even worse? My story was gunning for my complete emotional annihilation. Hold on, dear reader, this is where it goes from bad to worse.

Jack was the absolute sexiest thing I'd ever laid eyes on. His thick, curly hair was as dark as his eyes. And his swagger was so intense it would make you orgasm if you didn't shield your gaze. I was set up for failure right out of the gate.

For our first date we agreed to meet at a local bar for happy hour. A vodka martini marked my spot when I arrived.

"That's your drink, right?" he asked.

"Usually, yes. It's my opening pitch." I smiled coyly.

"But not tonight? I'll get you something else." He motioned for the bartender.

"No, no. It's perfect. Thank you."

One drink turned into three, and with no desire to eat, I left my soberness and inhibition on the barstool. We walked to another bar, laughing the entire way.

"You're such a bachelor," I said.

"What? Why would you say that?"

"Are you kidding me? Everything about you screams bachelor. I bet your house is a mess. I bet you never use your kitchen. I bet you only use your bathroom and, of course, your bedroom. Now *that* room gets the most use." I laughed raucously.

He stopped suddenly. I walked a few steps ahead and turned around. Our eyes locked, and there was no mistaking the lustful look in his eyes. I seductively sauntered toward him, ready to give him exactly what he wanted.

Before I knew it, we were in his bedroom completely naked. We kissed hard and fierce—my face rubbed raw from his stubble. I groped his body until his engorged manliness filled both my hands.

The next morning, I awoke thoroughly ashamed of my drunkenness and praying I could leave without waking him. Just as I was ready to slide stealthily off the bed, he grabbed my arm.

"Where do you think you're going?" He smiled playfully and tugged at my wrist.

I wanted to say, "Absolutely nowhere. Fuck me again." Instead, I said, "I'm so sorry about last night. Never order me martinis again."

"I'm ordering you martinis every night if this is what happens."

"You're not feeling all trapped and bachelor-ish?"

He sat up and kissed me tenderly. "Let's try this sober and see what happens."

We spent the first few weeks doing nothing but having sex. Okay, maybe that's an exaggeration, but only a bit of one. I couldn't believe it. It was like the Universe was making up for all the sex I hadn't had. It's as if it were saying, "Here's your crash course, girl, go for it!"

And I'll just say this . . . it was *good*.

We went on like that for a couple of months. Between all the sex, we ate at trendy restaurants. He drove me to the beach in his Porsche. He taught me about port and gave me books on Stoicism. He navigated every inch of my body with ease and pleasured me nightly while '70s hits strummed from the stereo.

I fell completely in love with him. I mean, flat-out "he's a god; I can't live without him" kind of love. What had started as an intense sexual relationship had seemingly blossomed into a full-fledged *relationship* relationship, something I didn't even think was possible for me. And one day, while basking in the glow of our afternoon delight, Jack said he loved me. I flinched. Some part of me knew that he might love me, in a way that a serial non-committer and long-time bachelor could, but it seemed like a miracle that a guy like Jack had suddenly changed his ways.

I was different, he said. Special. Someone he could really be with. Someone he could marry—maybe even have a baby with. And did I want to go to his parents' house on Sunday for spaghetti?

A baby *and* spaghetti? I was sunk.

While twirling my pasta that Sunday, I looked at Jack lovingly and relished in the fact that I was the one who changed him. I was the one who'd rescued this gorgeous man from all the loveless relationships he'd suffered through. All this and I was having mind-blowing sex? This was more than I ever thought possible for a woman who'd endured more beatings, experienced more abandonment, and did without love more than anyone she'd ever known. But none of that mattered anymore. I loved every way he touched me and every word he whispered in my ear. I was certain he loved me and that my days of being alone were over for good. I'd sacrifice all of me to make sure that this love, this relationship, lasted forever.

But before long, something in Jack was different. His eyes grew even darker. I could no longer discern my reflection, as dim as it was, in those deep, black lagoons. He'd locked me out good and tight. One Saturday, after a sexless morning, he asked me to leave. He wanted time alone to smoke cigars and read. The first time or two he asked this, I obliged sweetly and went back to my house, terrified to be alone. I hadn't ever really been alone, and the fears and memories of Mom and Dad that came up for me in those isolated times were too much for my fragile self to process. I was racked with desperation. Jack had called up my deepest, oldest story—abandonment.

When asking me to leave his house became a regular thing, my panic peaked. It didn't help that he often went out of town for work, or so he said, and that he didn't call me while he was gone. Someone hinted that he had a side piece, but I worried that *I* was the side piece and he'd grown tired of me. Besides my gnawing insecurities, he was all I had.

Most nights he was away, I paced my house, biting my cuticles and telling myself that he wouldn't cheat on me. I loved him too much for him to be unfaithful, right? Not knowing how to soothe myself, I chugged wine from an oversized glass that read "shopping is my cardio" and prayed he would call. When he didn't, I called him again and again until he answered.

One evening when I knew he was returning from a trip, I camped out on his front porch. I would finally confront him and make sure he knew I wouldn't stand for him ignoring me or lying to me. Nope. I was going to give him a piece of my mind. Maybe he just needed to know that he hurt me and then everything would be different. Wouldn't it?

A few minutes later, the roar of his car's German engine startled me. He whipped around the corner and into the driveway, his rapid downshift signaling his dark mood. From the porch I waved nervously. He didn't wave back. He pulled into the garage and closed the door. *Did he not see me? How could he not see me?*

At the front door, I shifted my weight nervously from one foot to another, my hand frozen in the knock position. *Just tell him how you feel. He'll say he's sorry, and everything will be okay.*

He flung the door open.

I jumped.

"What are you doing here?" he growled.

"Welcome home! I missed you."

"I'm really tired. It's been a long trip."

"You were only gone two days."

"Well, it's . . ."

I bit my lower lip. "When you go away, why don't you call me? Don't you miss me?" *Why was he not inviting me in?*

I stepped closer, trying to get a whiff of his intoxicating bravado.

He blocked the open doorway.

"I'm busy. Sometimes I'm too busy to call. And look, if you don't understand that, then we shouldn't be together."

I swallowed hard. My stomach was now as tight as a wrung-out towel. I couldn't be without him. What would I do without him? We were supposed to be together forever. He was the only person who'd ever really loved me. I couldn't screw this up.

Don't panic.

My eyes filled with tears. "What? No. No. No. I'm fine with you going away and being too busy to call me. I understand. I really do."

"I'm not sure you do. If I don't have time to call you or maybe I just don't feel like calling you, then I won't. It's that simple." He clenched his jaw, and his eyes clouded over. There wasn't one speck of sparkle—just like Mom's used to be.

"I get it. Please, I thought we were happy together. I don't want to break up. Give me another chance. Please." Tears rolled hot down my cheeks.

"Look, I'm really tired," he said.

"Sure." I looked at him longingly before starting down the steps to the driveway.

"Unless you want to come in?" He leaned through the doorway.

"Do you want me to come in?"

He lunged at me and kissed me deeply. Within seconds, his hand was up the leg of my shorts, his fingers thrusting inside me. My mind swirled with confusion, but the rest of me raged with ecstasy.

"What do you want me to do?" I whispered.

"Whatever I say."

We made love for hours that night, and as he wrapped his body around mine, he whispered, "God, I fucking love you. You're so sweet and sexy. Don't leave me, no matter what."

I pulled his arms tightly around me and exhaled. I couldn't lose him. I vowed to stay good and quiet and sweet and give him exactly what he wanted whenever he wanted it. I didn't consciously realize it at the time, but I was repeating the emotional pattern I'd established with Max and my parents before that—becoming dependent on someone who's emotionally unavailable, finding strange comfort in their unpredictability and abandonment, and when they inevitably hurt me, reinforcing my own story of unworthiness.

Jack and I went back to our old, lustful ways for a few weeks, but soon he was disappearing again. I did laps around my living room praying he'd call. When he didn't, I called him. Voicemail. Every time. *Doesn't he love me anymore?* I thought. *What did I do wrong? Why would he leave me? I did everything right.*

A week later he knocked on my door. I pulled back the curtain.

His face was nearly touching the glass. "Can I come in?"

I opened the door and backed away.

"I'm sorry. I know. I haven't called."

I wiped my running nose with the back of my hand. "I don't get what's happening here. I thought you loved me."

"I don't do love, long-term anyway. But I tried," he said.

I winced. He didn't love me after all. But I guess I was supposed to be thankful that he *tried*? "So, all the stuff about loving me forever and wanting babies, that was all a lie?"

"I showed you who I was, but you didn't leave."

"And you decided being mean and hurtful and cheating on me was the answer? You got a kick out of humiliating me. I'm so stupid. You've been treating me like this for months."

He smirked. "Well, you must like it."

"Like what?"

"How I treat you—you must like it. You don't sign up for this—" he drew an imaginary circle in between us "—unless you like crazy."

Something in me clicked. As terrified as I was of losing him, he'd hit my emergency eject button. "Crazy" was the adjective that scared me more than all the others I feared about myself. My mother was crazy, or so I'd told myself to make sense of all the beatings, and I would never be my mother. I opened the door and motioned for him to leave.

"I completely get it. And this . . ." I retraced his imaginary circle, ". . . we are done."

When the roar of his engine was finally in the distance, I trembled with the panic that most frequently rocked my body in the middle of the night. I locked the door and ran through the house, turning every light switch on and off and then on again, a habit formed in childhood after having the electricity turned off more than a few times. My face dripped with sweat, and I struggled to breathe. I cradled my cell phone in my hand and dialed nine and then one and then—was I dying? I clicked the phone off. Desperate to root myself in some form of present moment reality, I ran to the kitchen and chugged a bottle of cold water. I made my way to the bathroom and looked in the mirror.

Mom stared back at me.

Mascara was caked under my eyes, and my skin was dry and haggard. I was alone and unloved just like her. Oh my God, I *was* her. I put my finger down my throat and threw up. I hated her disgusting face and her desperation. No matter what I did, I couldn't escape her or her fucking dysfunction. I cradled the toilet bowl and sobbed, the smell of my vomit making me gag.

I drifted off to sleep later that night but sat bolt upright at 3 a.m. as if someone had pounded on my chest. Lying alone in bed, I ached with just as much self-loathing as those nights when Mom kept me awake for hours beating me and calling me names. Even all these years later, I could still taste the blood seeping from my cracked lips. It was my thirst for that old familial pain that drew me to men who would never love me. And I knew no matter how good and sweet and perfect I tried to be, even those who might dally with the idea of loving me would rather heave themselves into an abyss than stay with me.

In the months following my breakup with Jack, I was raw. Every inch of me ached. Even the air floating on my skin was too much to bear. When my friends called to check on me, I lied and told them I was fine and that it was all Jack's fault. I mean, what a jerk! He never intended on marrying me, and probably not anyone for that matter. But at night, when I was completely alone, I shivered with a knowing that I was to blame. I was unworthy of the only man I'd ever loved. I wasn't enough for him. How could I be? I wasn't even enough for myself.

HOW YOUR STORY TAKES OVER YOUR LIFE

Does this kind of pain feel familiar? Does my desperate masochism percolate a knowingness in your soul? Has your world at one point or another completely imploded? If so, then your story has taken over your life. At this point in your journey, you've likely pinpointed when and how your story began and the subtle yet profound power it gathered over time as it limited your life and entangled you in its misery. Like a hurricane, it brewed somewhere off in the distance, churning up emotional waves with every bit of turbulence you faced.

But with enough time and enough repetitive friction, your story became a force you could no longer control. And if we're being completely honest, its force became so intense, you didn't even try to control it. You couldn't. Its power transformed you into a non-thinking, illogical version of yourself that allowed your emotional brain to define who you are. Perhaps it propelled you into an abusive relationship? Maybe it sank you to the bottom of a tequila bottle or into a never-ending cycle of spending or gambling? Maybe it convinced you to lie when the truth would do as good?

The catastrophic effect of our stories takes shape when we allow them to run roughshod over us. When this happens, we don't know how to be anything other than brainwashed by our stories. Instead of taking control of the narrative and redirecting our energy and actions down a healthy path, we batten down the hatches and await the aftermath of our inaction and our near self-destruction. Tragically, we succumb to our past and all its limitations.

Just as there were various ways in which we got tangled up in our stories, there are just as many ways in which our stories take over our lives. Here are a few of the most destructive ways our stories control us.

WE BECOME ADDICTED TO PAIN AND CHAOS

Has your story shackled you to an unhealthy relationship? Or has it locked you into a string of dysfunctional relationships? Are you consistently attracted to the same type of person? Someone who ignores you? Plays emotional hide-and-seek? Abandons you, then swears they'll never do it again? Do you cling desperately to friends and lovers regardless of how they treat you because you're fearful of upsetting them? Perhaps you can't say no, thereby sacrificing your happiness for the sake of others? Do you walk around on eggshells to "keep the peace" and then blow up at the smallest incident?

If so, then you might be addicted to pain and chaos.

This is one of the most powerful ways our story takes hold of our lives. The discomfort of the pain and chaos becomes satisfying—and understandably so. This addiction stems from a chemical release of hormones that happens when our fight-or-flight response is triggered.

Earlier we learned that with ongoing trauma and chaos, we can get stuck in fight-or-flight overdrive. With enough time, this new chemical imbalance causes a disarrayed internal state that feels normal. We then subconsciously crave our internal chemical cocktail and the high it yields. In the book *The Body Keeps the Score*, Dr. Bessel van der Kolk writes about this gradual chemical adjustment and the gratification it creates. For some who have endured great trauma, he writes, "Fear and aversion, in some perverse way, can be transformed into pleasure."[34]

Just as with other addictions, when we don't get the "drug" we crave, we experience withdrawal,[35] often feeling anxious, restless, and bored. We seek that hit of excitement, and when we don't get it, we create it. This is why even if we find the most amazing new friend or lover, someone who's self-aware, kind, and emotionally intelligent, the relationship likely won't last. The normalcy of it will feel foreign and uncomfortable.

It is also common for those of us who endured childhood trauma to subconsciously adopt the dysfunctional patterns of our family of origin and reenact them in relationships. This behavior is caused by the mere-exposure effect, or being subconsciously drawn to what's familiar to us. Most of the time this means the more pain and chaos the better. When we don't have a relationship that brings drama or dysfunctional excitement, we fabricate it. We bristle up. We argue. We're needy and despairing. We're passive. Then aggressive. We're apathetic but silently filled with rage. We dole out the silent treatment on the regular. We panic. We're anxious. We're thoroughly sarcastic. We succumb to our story of worthlessness, and then out of sheer desperation, we give others every bit of ourselves hoping they won't leave us. This, in turn, leaves us emotionally depleted and resentful.

This is what happened to me. Maybe to you, too? My parents didn't show me what love was. They modeled violence and walking out when things got tough. While my father wasn't physically present, my mother abandoned me emotionally and abused me physically. For the most part, they weren't affectionate either, except with each other sexually, which likely explains the intense, familiar draw I had to Jack. Their routine abandonment split me emotionally into a maven hellbent on escape and a broken little girl whose unresolved, unspoken trauma left her frozen in a space-time continuum of chaos.

Jack, with all his emotional abandonment, felt like home to me, and the chaotic disarray of being with him became my drug of choice. Just like I craved our sex, something in me wanted every turbulent hit of drama the two of us could create. He also had something that fed my addiction more powerfully than sex and chaos—his routine abandonment reinforced the false stories I'd written about myself and my unworthiness. But an idea that subsequently surfaced during therapy—that I was more than that abandoned, unloved little girl—terrified me even more than being without Jack. That fear of being something greater, of having worth, is what left me tethered to my story for a while longer.

Do you want to find joy? Do you want your default internal setting to be one of peace instead of conflict? If we are to rid ourselves of our addiction to chaos, and even more so the delicious pain of it all, we must step out of the darkness and into the light of our being. Shifting our decision-making from the lowest parts of ourselves—the emotional brain—to our highest self—the thinking brain, where brilliant conscious awareness awaits—requires a non-negotiable desire to find pleasure from our peace instead of our pain.

OUR STORY TAKES A TOLL ON THE BODY

Another way our story takes over our life is through the toll it takes on our body. It is without question that unresolved trauma, stress, and suppressed emotions negatively affect our health. As early as 1892, Dr. William Osler, who's known as the father of modern medicine, discussed the connection between disease and emotional stress.[36]

Since then, various studies have found a connection between emotions and disease, and since the early 1990s, there have been studies confirming that chronic stress response is causally linked to the common cold, heart disease, autoimmune disorders, and cancer. One such study was the 1995 CDC and Kaiser Permanente Adverse Childhood Experiences (ACE) study that researched the correlation between childhood trauma and adult health risks and disease.[37]

In the study, Kaiser Permanente HMO members were asked whether they experienced childhood traumas, such as emotional, physical, or sexual abuse, and whether they witnessed drug or alcohol abuse or domestic violence.[38] The researchers reported that childhood trauma had an adverse impact on adult health and well-being, concluding that there was a "strong graded relationship between the breadth of exposure of abuse or household dysfunction during childhood and multiple risk factors for several of the leading causes of death in adults." Heart disease, cancer, chronic lung disease, skeletal fractures, and liver disease were among the causes of death reported.

How is this possible? Because our emotions impact us on a cellular level.

When we're triggered into fight or flight, nearly every cell in our body is flooded with cortisol, adrenaline, and proteins called cytokines. These chemicals cause inflammation, which weakens the immune system. With enough inflammation, a weak or stressed immune system can turn on itself, causing autoimmune disorders such as rheumatoid arthritis and multiple sclerosis. Or, in the case of cancer, errant cells run amok instead of initiating their own self-destruction through a process called apoptosis.

In his book *The Myth of Normal*, Dr. Gabor Maté, a world-renowned expert in the field of the stress-body connection, explains the connection between stress and disease. While he states that stress cannot "cause" cancer per se, "[S]tress plays its incendiary role: for example, through the release of inflammatory proteins into circulation—proteins that can instigate damage to DNA and impede DNA repair in the face of malignant transformation. These proteins, called cytokines, can also inactivate genes that would normally suppress tumor growth, enable chemical messengers that support the growth and survival of tumor cells, stimulate the branching of blood vessels that bring nutrients to feed the tumor, and undermine the immune system."[39]

The toll our emotional story takes on the physical body is further amplified when the trauma or stress is ongoing and our nervous system subsequently becomes dysregulated. Sometimes, due to mental and physical conditioning, dysregulation occurs even if the trauma stops. That is, we become stuck in a physical stress response because our mind and body have become conditioned to the previous or ongoing trauma. When this happens, the body continually emits inflammatory chemicals, shifting our homeostasis from peace to fear, alarm, and dis-ease.

Dr. van der Kolk reported his findings of this physiological state in *The Body Keeps the Score*, writing, "Under normal conditions people react to a threat with a temporary increase in their stress hormones. As soon as the threat is over, the hormones dissipate, and the body returns to normal. The stress hormones of traumatized people, in contrast, take

much longer to return to baseline and spike quickly and disproportionately in response to mildly stressful stimuli. The insidious effects
of constantly elevated stress hormones include memory and attention
problems, irritability, and sleep disorders. They also contribute to many
long-term health issues, depending on which body system is most vulnerable in a particular individual."[40]

Disease can also manifest when we suppress the emotions surrounding the trauma. In his book *When the Body Says No: Exploring the
Stress-Disease Connection*, Dr. Maté cites studies by the National Cancer Institute, which found that breast cancer patients who expressed their
anger and forged an "I will beat this" mentality had more active natural
killer immune cells in circulation than those patients who suppressed
their emotions.[41] Maté also writes, "In most cases of breast cancer, the
stresses are hidden and chronic. They stem from childhood experiences,
early emotional programming, and unconscious psychological coping
styles. They accumulate over a lifetime to make someone susceptible
to disease."[42] Undoubtedly, the negative charge of our unresolved emotions carries a high risk of significant disease.

A powerful and documented study of fear and the inflammatory turmoil it creates is discussed in Dr. Kelly Turner's book *Radical Remission: Surviving Cancer Against All Odds*.[43] The study was conducted to
test a new chemotherapy drug. The first group received the drug, while
the second, a control group, received a saline solution that they believed
was the chemo drug. Thirty percent of the control group lost their hair
even though they never received chemo. That's right—forty people were
so afraid of losing their hair, they scared themselves bald.

As it is for so many of us with unresolved trauma and trapped emotional energy, we live for years feeling unwell. For some, it's a diagnos-
able condition, the symptoms of which are managed with medication.

For others, it's more a general feeling of malaise, a sense that something just isn't right, but also something that a doctor can't identify with any certainty. While there is a time and place for Western medicine in relation to the diagnosis and treatment of physical ailments, there is also much to be said for gathering a fuller, more holistic picture of our emotional and mental landscape before dis-ease becomes disease.

When I see my integrative medicine doctor for checkups and bloodwork, she routinely asks me what is going on in my life. How have I been feeling emotionally? Have I gone through trauma? Do I feel anxious? How am I sleeping? What thoughts roll through my brain most often? Do I feel supported in my personal life? Am I resentful about anything? Am I sad? Unhappy? It's a powerful treatment protocol that addresses the deeper emotional and energetic aspects of physical health. I wish more doctors asked about a patient's past traumas and whether the emotions around that trauma were processed.

I See You

Later in the book, I'll share various modalities that will help you release the suppressed emotional energy of your story. But right now, I want to share an effective and easy exercise I use several times a day. I call it "I see you," which is a phrase I use when talking to my husband, friends, and dogs. It's how I convey that I see who they are, what they want, and how they feel. It's how I let them know that I value who they are to me. I've taken this powerful concept and applied it to my emotions. Let's give it a try.

When you feel an emotional storm brewing, when your anger, fear, rage, or disappointment is churned up, stop everything you're doing. Go somewhere quiet, close your eyes, and breathe deeply. Wait for those fiery emotions to get right up to the top of your being. Visualize them scurrying around frantically.

Then, in the most loving way you can, say, "I see you." And then wait. Breathe deeply a few times and check back in with your emotions.

If they're still buzzing around, ask them, "Why are you so upset, my sweet?" Then breathe and wait until the answer appears.

When the reason is clear, show compassion. "Now I know why you're here and what you're trying to protect me from. *I see you*. I honor you and I thank you."

Then visualize the emotions flowing from your body just as they flowed in. Let the emotions flow in and out, over and over again, until your body is washed clean of them. With practice, you will begin to see that your emotions are not the truth. They are not you, and they are not the situation. Your emotions are an expression of your interaction with life. They are meant to be felt and released—never, ever suppressed.

This is how we shift from our emotional brain to our thinking brain. This awareness creates the pivot point needed to stop being the victim of our emotions and instead be the conscious curator of a peaceful and happy inner landscape. This is how we keep our story from taking a toll on our body.

OUR STORY STARVES THE SOUL

Our story also takes over our life when it starves our soul of happiness and purpose. As sure as I am about anything in this life, I know we are here to feel joy. Exhilaration and inner peace are on the menu for everyone. We're also here to do our soul's work—to honor the Divine in us while gleefully getting our hands dirty and our feet wet. It is in those moments of sifting the earth through our fingers and playing in puddles

WHEN YOUR STORY TAKES OVER YOUR LIFE   133

that life is calling us to the light of our being. Our purpose here is not to suffer and feel unworthy. It is to feel limitless joy and elevate others with our greatest gifts. It is to love deeply and profoundly. To feel our worth with such splendor that we can't help but share our light with others.

When we allow our stories to take over our lives, we close off the brilliant light of our soul. It has no refuge from the internal turmoil raging through us. And so it bucks up. A little bit here and a little bit there, shaking us gently at first, hoping a nudge will remind us of our intended grandeur. When that doesn't work, it rattles us with a bit more force, hoping to jar us back to our life's mission. In our physical body we feel more than uneasy. We feel conflicted, constantly searching for something we can't identify. We're lost in the depth of our own being. We're ravenous but never satiated. Our soul is begging to be heard.

. . . .

After my breakup with Jack, I'd slink back home after work, turn on the TV, and drink at least one, sometimes two, bottles of wine. Nothing soothed my pain. After months of anxiety and continued inner turmoil, I caught on that there wasn't enough alcohol in the world to numb my pain. I decided I'd have to fix myself.

Somehow.

I spent the next six months alone. I saw people at work and went out with friends here and there, but I did not date. I wanted to learn how to be comfortable being alone or, better yet, understand why I couldn't bear being alone. I needed the memories of Mom and Dad to stop before the past extinguished the last bit of my being.

There was a restless part of me—my soul—that craved more and desired less.

More peace, less anger. More love, less hate. More joy, less apathy.

I saw a therapist and read a lot of books. I learned to meditate. I journaled and signed up for yoga. Before long, I saw that my crushing agony wasn't about my breakup with Jack—it was about my breakup with myself. I had a cavern of unresolved trauma that had not only disassociated me from the world but had cut me off from the Divine inside me and who I was here to be.

The deeper I got into myself and into therapy, I realized that I didn't know how to resolve my trauma, soothe my pain, or comfort myself. I didn't have the tools. As a little girl, I'd never been taught how to comfort myself, nor was I afforded the space to talk through my pain. So of course, I didn't know how to comfort myself after a breakup that felt like the *Titanic* hitting that fateful iceberg. And I certainly wasn't equipped, even as a thirty-three-year-old woman, to soothe myself from the countless traumas of abuse, neglect, and abandonment I'd endured.

Learning how to soothe myself without alcohol, sex, or other distractions would take everything I had. But my soul had sounded the alarm. There was only one thing to do if I was ever going to find the light. I had to go back into that dark place and resolve all my old trauma once and for all.

LET'S SUM IT UP

There are countless ways our stories take over our lives. With each bit of friction and turbulence we face, our stories are reinforced, proving to ourselves yet again that we are indeed unworthy of peace, joy, and love. Because of our unresolved trauma and the dysfunctional patterns created in our family of origin, we may be addicted to pain and chaos.

As a result, we'll choose unhealthy relationships and unfulfilling careers that reinforce our perceived limitations.

Our story also takes over our life through the toll it takes on our physical health. When we live with unresolved trauma and its emotional energy, dis-ease forms in our body, with some of us developing full-blown disease. Our story also takes over our life by starving our soul. We desire more but settle for less, which leaves us feeling restless and off-kilter. If we are going to free ourselves from our story's grasp, we must develop an awareness of our emotions and learn to release them with grace while soothing ourselves with love.

NOW IT'S YOUR TURN

Here we are, back to this beautiful time when we go deeper into your journey and uncover the various ways in which your story took over your life. Remember, this is not about blaming and judging. This part of healing is about witnessing the events and circumstances of your life. Awareness is also key here for tuning into your body and how it feels. If you can tap into that unresolved trauma and see how your story has taken over your life, you can save yourself from mental, emotional, physical, and spiritual dis-ease.

Sit somewhere quiet—a cozy place where you feel safe. Take a few deep breaths and trust that what shows up for you when reading these questions is meant to be here. This is a significant step in healing your oldest wounds and connecting to the Divine in you.

How was love modeled to you as a child?

Did your parents argue or fight often? Did you witness or experience physical violence or abuse?

When you experienced trauma, did you talk to anyone about it? Were you comforted?

Were you taught how to soothe yourself when you felt pain, discomfort, or trauma?

When you're upset now, how do you make yourself feel better? Do you drink, smoke, take drugs, or shop excessively?

What type of people are you choosing in relationships?

What patterns do you see?

Do you sacrifice yourself to make others happy?

Can you say no without guilt if you don't want to do something?

Do you panic, think the worst, act clingy, pick fights, or constantly question your partner's intentions?

Do you withdraw emotionally and mentally from your partner, zoning out for periods of time?

Do you lose your temper? Are you overly critical? Do you unintentionally reenact any witnessed chaos from your childhood?

Do you go with the flow, then blow up at the slightest incident?

Do you feel panicked? Anxious? Unsure about your place in life?

Do you sleep well?

Do you express your emotions or suppress them?

If something or someone upsets you, do you talk about it?

Do you feel resentment, anger, or rage but choose not to be emotionally forthright?

Are you sarcastic with family and friends?

Have you been taught that sarcasm is an acceptable form of relating to one another?

Are you currently having health issues?

Does your medical doctor conduct an emotional and mental well-being checkup with you?

Who do you talk to when you need to get something off your chest?

Do you feel uneasy or uncomfortable? Conflicted? Unfulfilled?

Is there a part of you that yearns for inner peace and self-worth, but you don't know how to get there?

Awareness, as you know, is always the first step in healing. It's taking the emotional brain's story and sending it upstairs to the thinking brain for insight and conscious compassion. I hope you see that it's your unresolved trauma and resulting story that have taken over your life, leaving you steeped in untruths about your worthiness. The Divine part of you wants to be free from this pain and your old stories. It can be scary to tune into that grand part of you that craves freedom when all you've ever known is limitation. But the beauty of what lies ahead for you is worth it.

Come with me, won't you? We're off to extract our true selves, the part of us that's pure and glorious and worthy of whatever we desire.

8

. . . .

EXTRACTING YOUR TRUE SELF AND RELEASING THE STORY

Wearing my old law school sweatshirt, with my hair in a top knot that looked as disheveled as my insides felt, I plopped heavily onto the therapist's cold leather couch. Even though her smile was warm and welcoming, I folded my arms across my chest in subconscious defiance. I resented being there despite the fact that I'd begged for her soonest appointment.

I told her about the anxiety, panic, and the relentless resurfacing of my most traumatic memories. I intended to tell her about my breakup with Jack as well, but my childhood memories, furious and precise, were raising hell inside me most nights of the week.

"And what are those memories?" she asked.

"Bad stuff."

"Such as?"

"Just your run-of-the-mill bad childhood stuff."

"Can you tell me more?"

"I had bad parents. But hey, I mean, doesn't everybody?"

"No. No, actually, they don't."

"Well, I did. I don't want to talk about the details. What I want is for you to tell me how to make it stop. Help me forget it all. It was so long ago. There's no reason for me to think about it anymore. And help me sleep, please. I can hardly function anymore."

"All these memories are coming up now because it's time to finally release the energy surrounding them. I'm sensing you've not done that."

She explained that to survive as a child and later succeed as an adult, I suppressed my emotions, unable or unwilling to process them. Now that there was perceived space and safety in my life, my subconscious inner child was spewing out old, unprocessed emotions like an erupting volcano.

"Your inner little girl is righteously pissed off. Her feelings can't be pushed down forever," she said.

A vision of six-year-old me flashed in my mind. Pigtails. Shorts. A long-sleeved striped shirt. Sweeter eyes than I remembered. Then, she stuck her tongue out at me.

"The dreams, the panic attacks—they're all clear indicators that that part of you is demanding to be heard."

I squirmed and kept my mouth shut, swallowing back a big, hard "NO!" No, I wasn't about to relive those memories. If they terrified me that much just glimpsing them at 3 a.m., what would they do to me if I brought them into the light of day? This inner little girl of mine would have to crawl back into the place I'd created for her shameful self—that dark part of me where no one could see her. I'd fought hard not to be her anymore, and I didn't need her coming around to remind me of who I used to be.

The therapist tapped her pen on the table. "I suggest you pay attention to her. Give her a safe space and listen. And then . . . maybe try to love her? Sounds to me like she could use a little love."

As if turning over the mic to the younger, abandoned me wasn't bad enough, the therapist then suggested the unthinkable.

"After we hear from the little one, there's some forgiveness work I suggest we do."

I glared at her.

"All this hostility you're carrying around about your parents—"

"You mean this *justified* hostility?" I countered incredulously.

"It's not doing you any favors. Accepting your trauma without shame and forgiving those involved are both necessary steps in true healing."

Back home, I flopped my exhausted body on the bed and closed my eyes. Was my therapist right? Had I suppressed all my old emotions? Avoided processing my trauma?

Did my inner little girl need to be heard? What did she want to say? Could I ever forgive Mom and Dad for their abuse and neglect? How, after all these years of pain, could I finally find true healing? It was overwhelming to even consider the work I had ahead of me. But I knew, without a doubt, what I had to do first: rid myself of my shame.

I was so ashamed of the poor, violent place I came from. I was even more ashamed of everything I'd done to survive it. But if I wanted to heal, I'd have to extract my true self—the authentic me, without the baggage of my past—and release the story I'd written because of my trauma.

· · · · · · · · · · · · · · · ·

Extracting our true self is a crucial step in releasing our stories. It is what will empower us to finally rise above the story that's limited our lives.

There are four steps in extracting our true self:

1. Ridding ourselves of shame.
2. Soothing our inner child.
3. Forgiving those who wronged us.
4. Forgiving ourselves and grieving our stories.

Accomplishing each step is how you will release your story once and for all. This was, without question, the most challenging work I'd done, but it was so worth it. After decades of anguish, I finally released the chokehold of my old stories.

I promise you this—if I can do it, you can, too.

RIDDING OURSELVES OF SHAME

Shame is one of the biggest reasons we live inside our limiting stories for so long. It's also a powerful and deadly emotion. After experiencing trauma, we can get caught up in a shameful story that says we are to blame or that because this happened to us, we are eternally wounded or, even worse, broken. There's an inner voice that tells us we're not enough and that we're unworthy of a beautiful life. Shame also mandates our silence. Under its purview, we are forbidden to speak of what happened or how it made us feel. And who would care anyway, right?

That's what shame wants you to believe. Shame is the nectar of the devil himself. It will seduce you, insidiously promising protection from the world. *No one will ever know what happened.* With enough time, shame takes over our being. We no longer resonate with who we really are. We forget who we wanted to be, where we wanted to go, and how to truly love ourselves.

All we know is what feels like the dirty, secret bits of ourselves.

After seeing the therapist who encouraged me to love my inner little girl, it took me ten more years to fully unravel my shame. An entire decade! My pain and anger were too much for me at times, and I'd slide back into shame mode, afraid to talk about what my inner little girl and I went through. I didn't tell my friends or David, the man who would later become my husband. I mistakenly believed that if I did, they would abandon me. I was a grown woman still clinging to a false story that if I were my true self, if others knew about my past, they wouldn't love me.

Shame is, without question, a deadly emotion. It will keep you from love. It will beat you down harder than any abuse you endured. It will choke the life right out of you while the sun shines brightly through your kitchen window.

I should know. It nearly killed me until something quite unexpected happened that ultimately released the floodgates of my repressed shame.

. . . .

When I was forty-three, my beloved golden retriever, Finn, was diagnosed with cancer. He was only seven, and he loved me unconditionally. He was the first true love of my life. As the Universe would have it, Finn died nearly twenty years to the day that my mom died of cancer. On his march toward death, with every drop of chemo and holistic remedy, I'd slide back in time, reliving my old traumas and the shame that went along with them.

Finn knew the sadness I carried. He'd lie on me when I couldn't get out of bed and lick away my tears. And for all the years I knew this magnificent creature, I never understood why he loved me so much. I didn't have his magical ability to create happiness. I didn't believe in the inherent goodness of people and the possibilities of life. Mom didn't teach me any of that. She didn't teach me that the world was big enough to explore but small enough to conquer. She didn't teach me to believe in anything, much less myself.

In the last days of Finn's life, I wiggled into his warmth and dove deeper into my soul. I wondered if it was even possible for me to have a heart full of hope and belief instead of anger and shame. I squeezed Finn with all my might and opened my eyes. I knew the kind of healing I was considering would be hard work, but for the first time I didn't cower under the weight of my shame, nor did I tuck it away and ignore it. I brought it to the surface and let it flow out of me.

"Finn, my mom had a nasty, mean cancer too. She died when she was so young—forty-four—the age I will be soon. She didn't have a big heart like you. She never had a light in her eyes, even when she was well. She wasn't much of a mother and did a lot of terrible things." I swallowed hard. "And, she nearly killed me—with her hands and her words."

The vibration of my vocal cords released the stifled energy in my throat. I'd never said those words aloud before. I sighed and then Finn sighed, and the restriction around my heart loosened for the first time in years. After Finn died, I took the rest of my shame (and all my stories) to my husband. I laid my head in his lap and bit by bit, tear by tear, I told him every shameful thing inside of me.

Releasing shame's death grip requires you to do the simplest thing in the most difficult way. You must talk about it. Find someone you trust—a therapist, a coach, a friend, your spouse. And then in that safe space, let it out. All of it. Do you know the most amazing thing about speaking your "dirty" stuff out loud? When you speak it, it's not dirty at all! It's victorious and clean. It's the most courageous part of you bubbling effervescently to the surface. Releasing that toxic energy from your body leaves you spiritually free. When we finally speak our shame, we aren't hiding who we really are anymore. We're finally free to be everything we're here to be.

SOOTHING OUR INNER CHILD

The next step in extracting your true self is to soothe your inner child. If you have suppressed emotions from childhood, it's likely that you weren't effectively comforted after trauma occurred, nor were you taught how to soothe yourself. As a result, in adulthood, we're ill-equipped to effectively acknowledge and process our emotions. Instead, we subconsciously suppress our emotions and numb our pain with food, alcohol, drugs, sex, shopping, gambling, or anything else that will distract from our distress. But the energy of those emotions—sadness, anger, rage, fear, shame, and grief—doesn't disappear. It stays trapped in our bodies, seeping into every cell of our being. Day after day we resonate with our emotional dis-ease as we write the ongoing story of our unworthiness.

Every therapist I saw agreed that the part of me that doubted my purpose and place in the world was born from my deeply traumatizing childhood. I was a sane and intelligent forty-three-year-old woman. But I harbored the unresolved trauma of the emotional and physical abuse I endured as a child, leaving me perpetually wounded. More than one therapist recommended inner child work to soothe and comfort that angry, abused part of me. They suggested I resolve my underlying feelings of anger and shame so I could feel whole. But to do that, the little, younger version of me needed to be heard. She had to, once and for all, release her suppressed emotions.

It's important to note here that the nature of inner child work is not objective, meaning that what unfolds in this work is highly personal, unique, and historic in nature. What surfaces will vary from person to person, whether that be splintered memories or charged emotions that get dislodged from the emotional brain's narrative loop. The goal is to make an authentic connection with that part of you, that wounded younger piece of your being, that needs to be heard and, most importantly, consoled.

Sometimes in therapy when I invited my inner little girl to share her angst, she came in like a wrecking ball, her honest blows bringing me to tears. I hated her for reminding me of my shortcomings. I hated her for bringing up Mom and Dad so much. The adult me wanted desperately to forget what they did and didn't do. But this younger version of me, the little girl who shouldered so much pain and responsibility for so many years, didn't get what she really needed—comfort and mothering from the adult me. I didn't thank her for what she did or encourage her to speak. I was still ashamed of what we lived through, and I didn't know how to care for this inner child of mine who was still, after all these years, full of rage. My inner little girl wanted to rebel and be free, but the adult, perfectionist, people-pleaser me wanted her to shut up and hide from the world.

After many therapy sessions, and not finding much common ground with the little one, I wondered if she and I needed some alone time. Perhaps in the comfort of home, I could bring us together in a way that felt more natural and unconstrained by appointment times. I'd learned about an exercise called compassion meditation, where you visualize

someone you'd like to feel compassion for or establish a deeper relationship with. The practice suggests starting with a clear, definitive picture
of the person in your mind, then imagine the difficulties they may have
experienced. Then, to round out the practice, you offer them peace or a
blessing. Could it really be that easy? Something told me it wouldn't be,
but I gave it a shot anyway.

The first few times I tried compassion meditation, I couldn't find
my inner little girl. Finn's spirit appeared instead. He'd passed away a
month before, but he was still with me in my dreams and meditations,
always running clumsily toward me over a splendid grassy knoll. I'd
squeeze him and the two of us would collapse in a field of wildflowers.
I rested in his comfort and asked that the next time he help me find my
inner little girl. Oh, how she loved dogs. Perhaps she'd trust Finn to
accompany her into the core of our shared angst.

One afternoon a few days later, I wrapped myself in the blanket
strewn at the end of my bed and went looking for my inner little girl.
Finn was there again.

"Hello, my love." I kissed him smack on the lips.

His spirit grabbed mine and said, *She's here.*

Various versions of the younger me clicked like the second hand of
a clock. Afraid. Hungry. Alone. Abandoned. Ashamed.

Don't be ashamed. Feel compassion for her . . . for yourself.

"I don't know, Finn. I can't break away from these memories. I think
they've wrecked me for good."

Come with me. Let me show you something.

He took off ahead, his energy guiding me until we were together in
my mind's eye, journeying back in time. My mind swirled and whirled,
flying me over Midwestern streets and lanes and picnic-blanketed
parks. In the driveway of the old ranch house, my green-and-white

bike was perched on its kickstand. My heart grew warm, and a smile spread across my cheeks. Maybe there was a happy time or two when the evening air smelled of summer rain and dancing lightning bugs lit my path.

I followed Finn deeper into the past, pausing over the rusty, abandoned steel mills and Dad's old car lot. I poked my head inside Dad's garage, the scent of gooey Bondo filling my nose. My favorite glass-bottle pop machine still tingled my senses from the dark, dingy corner.

Come on, Finn said. *We're almost there.*

The light ahead of us grew into a fluffy cloud, inviting us to its intangible core. With a whoosh, I was sitting on the couch in my old basement apartment. Mom and Dad were in the kitchen. The sounds of a crash and a smash and a few cuss words rolled down the hallway. I looked out the window as a woman walked by outside. From our basement vantage point, only her long wrap skirt, vinyl platform sandals, and freckled shins came into view. I curled my toes in the blue shag carpet. How I hated living below the sidewalk, where it seemed people walked on us all day long.

Then the entire apartment shook with Mom and Dad's anger. Windows rattled. Glasses broke. Mom's mirrored wallpaper peeled off the living room walls. When it stopped, the apartment looked just as it did the day Mom gave away my puppy.

"You're my very best friend, Whoopsie. Forever and ever, okay?" Little six-year-old me was holding Whoopsie, my small fingers lost in mounds of crinkly white fur. He was smaller than I remembered, but lying next to little me, he was larger than life.

"Oh, Whoopsie, I missed you!" My voice cracked with joy.

Just as little me was about to nuzzle him, there was a knock on the door, and a gray-haired woman appeared, her vulture-like claws clutching at Whoopsie.

Little me froze. The woman grabbed Whoopsie right out of her arms. "Mommy!" little me cried. "She's got Whoopsie! Mommy! What's she doing? Where's she going? Whoopsie! Don't let her take—"

Adult me looked away—I already knew how this ended. I couldn't bear to see Whoopsie leave again. Mom closed the door. Little me stretched past her with all her might to reach the chain across the door.

"Hurry! Open it," adult me yelled. "Look at him one more time . . . before it's too late."

Little me flung open the door until the locked chain stopped it. Squeezing her face through the opening, she yelled, "Whoopsie! Don't go. Don't leave me!"

Mom pulled her by the pigtail and shut the door. "Enough!" Then she click-clacked in her Dr. Scholl's sandals down the hall to the kitchen.

Little me threw herself on the couch and wailed. I felt every speck of pain she did. And again, it was unbearable, just like when Finn died. She needed comfort and love, not one of Mom's burnt bologna sandwiches. I knelt beside her.

"I know this hurts," I said.

"You don't care about me," she replied.

"Yes, I do. And I know how you feel right now . . . like someone reached in and tore your heart out. Like you're going to be alone forever because Whoopsie was your only friend and the only creature on the Earth who loved you."

She stood up and stared straight through me, teeter-tottering from her toes to her heels. I reached for her hand. She backed away.

I sat down, putting more space between us. "I'm trying to make us better. Why do you make it so hard for me to love you?"

"No one loves me, why should you? I'm ugly and stupid and my hair is colored like a mouse's. I don't have any friends except Sally, the old lady upstairs who gives me books that I don't understand. I don't know how to play or throw a ball or do kid things."

"But you know how to read, and Sally gives you those books because you're smart. She wants you to understand them. See?"

"And Mommy doesn't love me. She makes marks on my arm and pulls my hair. And sometimes she says she's sorry I was born."

Tears filled my eyes. I looked at her beautiful, round face and blinked, sending my sadness for her—for us—rolling down my cheeks.

Her face softened. She cupped her small palms on my cheeks, catching my tears, and then she made fists. "There, I took your tears. You don't have to be sad."

I opened her hands and rubbed her salty palms with my thumbs. "You don't have to do that for me. I'm not Mom."

She bit her lip, trying not to cry.

"I'm not sorry you were born. But I am sorry Mom was mean to you. I'm sorry Whoopsie was stolen from you. I'm sorry for all the times you had to be a big girl when you were supposed to be a little girl."

"Why did you leave me? Why did you grow up and do stupid things and forget all about me?" she asked.

"You're right. I wasn't there for you when you needed me."

"You were ashamed of me. You called me names. And all I wanted was to love you."

I rolled my eyes. "Really? It sure didn't feel like that. What about when you kept me up all hours of the night with your nonsense, making me think I was crazy?"

"I didn't mean to. I just wanted to be with you. I wanted you to love me."

"But sometimes you're scared and jealous and needy. And you don't know this yet, but if you're ever going to have a healthy relationship, you can't be like that."

"But how are we supposed to know if someone really loves us unless they see all of us?"

She had a point.

"I want to have fun," she said. "We never got to have fun, you know? Me and you."

"I know."

"We didn't roller-skate enough."

"I know."

"And we didn't get to play with Whoopsie enough. I miss him so much, my whole body hurts."

"I know. Mine too. And I'm so sorry we lost our Finn. I wish I could've saved him."

"You did good," she said, gazing downward.

More sadness rolled from my eyes and hers. Then in a shared instant, we put our hands on each other's cheeks.

"Maybe we can miss them together?" I asked.

"Maybe." She tied her pigtails in a knot under her chin. "Mommy died, too. Do you ever miss her?"

"What? No. Of course not. Do you?"

"I don't know. Sometimes. She was sad a lot; but when she was happy, she did silly things that made me laugh."

"Such as?" I asked.

"Like how she'd chew a half a piece of Doublemint gum and throw the other half in her purse without a wrapper. Then later, she'd ask me to get her the other half out of the bottom of her purse—"

"You mean that huge, dirty purse that she'd carry around with unwrapped cookies and crackers in it?"

"Yeah! And the gum would be all yucky and have old crumbs stuck to it. And she'd just pop it in her mouth like this." She opened her mouth and air-dropped an imaginary piece of gum in it. Then she doubled over in laughter.

I raised an eyebrow.

"It's so gross! Isn't it gross?" She could not stop laughing.

I shrugged.

"No wonder you never have any fun. You're too mad," she said.

"What? I am not."

"Yes, you are. Mommy's gone. She can't hurt us anymore. Maybe we'd have more fun if you weren't so mad at her all the time."

Really? Was this little twerp ever going to stop telling me what to do?

"And Finn really wants us to stop being mad at her. He told me so."

Her eyes glistened not with sadness but with hope that tomorrow would be lighter and happier than all of our yesterdays. Maybe she had a point.

"You know, I'd do anything for Finn . . . and for Whoopsie . . . and for you." Then she fell into me with pure elation and wrapped her arms around my neck.

"After you're done being mad at Mommy, can we go roller-skating and play with dogs?"

I squeezed her with all my might. "Anything you want."

We had a lot more work to do, the little one and I. But on that random winter afternoon, wrapped in an old blanket, I *saw* her. I heard her. And I loved her for the first time, ever. But more than anything, I was so proud of her and everything she did to ensure we survived.

It took us a couple more years to get our boundaries straight. She had to learn that I didn't need her stepping into arguments with her spiteful words and rageful ways. I taught her that her anger was nothing more than her old story of fear and abandonment resurfacing. That really, she craved love and a safe, warm embrace. It was also time for her to be the kid she never got to be. I would handle the adult stuff. All she had to do was have fun and bring me along.

Learning how to self-soothe is one of the most beautiful gifts you can give yourself. These days when I feel wounded, I meditate, pray, go on a walk, or do yoga. Other times, I find a quiet space and practice compassion meditation. Sometimes I visualize my inner little girl and sometimes I see me, just as I am now—a middle-aged woman who is worthy of compassion, love, and the rest of my days filled with limitless joy.

FORGIVING THOSE WHO WRONGED US

The next step in extracting our true selves and releasing our stories is to forgive those who've wronged us. Does just the idea of it make you bristle up, cringe, or yell, "hell no!"? If so, I get it. Forgiveness is hard, especially when someone abused, neglected, or abandoned you. A lot of why we refuse to forgive stems from the pesky emotional brain, which we now know interprets events, forms memories, and writes a story about those events and memories. When we process life from that place, we get caught up in victim mode, portraying a false sense of valor about the pain that was inflicted on us. We want to be "right" when, really, we should strive for inner peace.

We can get to forgiveness if we shift our thought processing from the emotional brain to the thinking brain. As we've learned, we do this by discerning the origin of the story (the trauma) from the story that our emotional brain wrote about it. We remind ourselves that the trauma was an event. We are not the trauma. It is what we experienced. We get to choose what we do and how we feel in its aftermath. This, my friends, is how we shift into conscious awareness. It's also how we find the compassion we need to forgive those who wronged us.

I didn't think I'd ever find forgiveness for the two people who were supposed to protect me yet abandoned and abused me repeatedly. Even when Mom was days from death, I couldn't find an ounce of compassion for her.

. . . .

Dad's voice booming down the hallway startled me. He was back again? When he learned that Mom didn't have long to live, he'd show up here and there, even though they were divorced, and chat her up about the old days. They'd reminisce and laugh about their worn-out Red Foxx albums. It was crazy to me that these two, who had, for decades, relished in completely gutting one another, would want to now share a chuckle about the old guy from *Sanford and Son*. And did Dad really have to be here on my twenty-fourth birthday? Couldn't I just have one day without these two screwing it up?

When I got to Mom's room, she was sitting up and wearing a T-shirt that had once fit snug across her voluptuous chest. It was now draped over her bony legs, which were dangling over the side of the bed. It'd been nearly two months since she last sat up on her own. I stood in the doorway frozen with disbelief. Dad sat snugly next to her.

"Come here," she whispered and patted the bed beside her.

I walked slowly toward her.

"Happy birthday to my first . . . born." Her exhaustion extended every syllable.

"Mom, how are you sitting up like this?"

"I feel better today. And Dad brought a cake for your birthday."

"I hate my birthday." My stomach tightened with anticipation. *What is happening?*

"Having you was—" She wobbled forward. Dad steadied her shoulders. "It wasn't easy, and . . . I did what I could." She took a long, labored breath. "Do you understand?"

I didn't understand. I did not understand why she beat me senseless all those times or why, for most of my life, she checked out and made me parent her children. And I didn't understand this absurd conversation and why we were having it now. After all these years and all the awful stuff she did to me, did she honestly think I would just let it all go? I couldn't do it, even if death was asking me to. I was furious with her—not to mention with God and life.

Dad chimed in. "Your mother asked you a question."

"Don't talk to me like I'm a child. I haven't been a child in, well, let me see . . . ever?"

"Don't be like that in front of your mother, she's—"

"Dying? Yeah, I know. She's been doing that for a while now, long before you showed up with your Redd Foxx stories."

"She's trying to tell you—"

"It's hard," Mom said. "You'll see what I mean." She coughed and winced in pain. I glanced at the morphine on the dresser but didn't reach for it.

"What your mother is trying to say is that—"

"Don't speak for her. If she has something to say, let her say it."

I stood firmly in my spot, waiting for her to say all the happy-ending movie things I had wanted her to say my whole life—that she loved me, that she was sorry for all of it, for beating me, for giving away my puppy, for spending all our money, for making me take care of the whole family. And, most of all, that if she could make it all different, she would.

Mom reached for my hand. I took hers instinctually because that's what beaten down, abused children do. Then, just as quickly, I dropped it. She was oblivious to my inner turmoil.

"Maybe I've turned the corner and I'm getting better?" Mom smiled like she was suddenly pain free for the first time in months. "Maybe tomorrow we can go shopping, you know, like the old days when things were good. We'll get some new clothes, and I'll need a couple of wigs, big ones like Diana Ross."

It all sounded so believable. I didn't know if she was serious or hallucinating. But all I could think was that even on her deathbed, Mom was all about the aesthetics.

"I miss those early days in the ranch house with you and your father," she told me with a sigh. "Disco music and riding around in the convertible. My hair blowing in the wind." She rubbed her scruffy head. "I must look terrible, huh?" She looked sheepishly at her lap.

"You look beautiful," Dad said.

"It's been a long ride," she said, inching her way back farther on the bed. "I'm tired."

"I know, honey." Dad helped her scooch all the way back.

As she lay down, she moaned and turned toward me. "Tomorrow we'll go shopping. Do this whole thing over. Dress up. Dance. Feel the wind."

"I can't wait. You know how much I loved the old days." I prayed she felt every drop of my sarcasm.

"I'm going to sleep. We have a big day tomorrow." She closed her eyes.

Dad stayed with her for a few minutes before coming out to the kitchen where I was washing the dishes.

"I'm taking off," he said.

And with a slam of the door and a gust of cold air, Dad was gone. This wasn't the first time he walked out, but I knew it would be the last. He didn't come back to see Mom again after that. Maybe he'd said all he needed to say. Or maybe once around the block with Mom was enough. I watched him back out of the driveway and then threw my birthday cake in the trash.

. . . .

Facing the truth that I had never been mothered was as traumatic as watching the woman who gave me life, and then nearly beat it out of me, die on my watch. There was no longer a chance to talk about it. To understand it. To mend it. She took that last little bit away from me the day she died. I felt I would never get closure. In those days leading up to her death, I mistakenly believed that if she answered my questions, if she told me why she abandoned and abused me, I could find peace and forgive her. As a twenty-four-year-old traumatized woman, I didn't understand that forgiveness was not about Mom or how she might explain away her wrongdoings. I didn't know that forgiveness was about me and how I would ultimately process what had transpired between us.

I harbored my unresolved feelings for Mom for decades. But as much as I pushed them down, my anger, rage, grief, and shame bubbled up. I walked through life temperamental and bitter. I wore my misery like a bulletproof vest. No one could get beyond it and into my heart. Was I going to live the rest of my life in the emotional shallow end because my mother wounded me? Was she worth the daily misery I endured? Was I going to let her manipulate and control me from the grave?

I had to forgive her once and for all. Maybe then I'd find peace.

Since my compassion meditation technique worked so well with my inner little girl, I decided to try it with Mom. Even if my heart couldn't find a speck of compassion for this woman, perhaps my soul could. I sunk deep into the chair, wrapped my favorite blanket around me, and closed my eyes.

"Mom? Are you there?"

And as if she were answering my call, her energy swelled inside me. I was transported to a day when I was about a year old, lying in my crib. My emotional memory recalled that I was hungry and crying. I can't explain where this thought came from or whether it was a real memory, but its effect was so emotionally overpowering, it was as if it'd just happened yesterday.

Mom paced the floor.

My hunger roared—*feed me*.

"Shut up!" she screamed. She squeezed my cheeks, her fingernails digging into my skin.

Then she walked away, leaving little me in the crib alone.

"You were never good about anything, let alone feeding me," I called after her. "At least when Dad was around, he made sure I ate."

Then I remembered a story Dad told me when I was about seven years old. He said it all took place when I was a baby, maybe a year old. He hadn't seen Mom since he pushed her out of his car when she was pregnant with me. But one day, Mom called him from a pay phone. Sobbing, she said she missed him and wanted us to be a family. Ten minutes later he pulled up to the pay phone. He took us to his basement apartment, where I ate every bit of food he gave me.

He said Mom and I moved in that day and ended his story by saying, "That's how much I loved your mother."

At seven years old, I didn't know what he meant. But putting all the pieces together decades later, I wondered if Dad took us in because he loved Mom, but Mom only stayed because she knew we couldn't survive without him.

Suddenly their story wasn't so different from my own. I, too, had made choices based on need and circumstance—and survival. Could I judge them for the decisions they made?

I sure as hell could because there's no way their dysfunctional, controlling, abusive behavior could possibly be love.

Could it?

I mean, maybe through the broken lens by which they viewed life it was the only kind of love they knew.

My soul chimed in to resolve my mental conflict. *They know only what they know. You are safe. Everything is as it should be. Let it out.*

Then rage roared through me.

"This was your favorite place, wasn't it, Mom? Lying around, despondent, depressed, oh, woe is you. Flushing the toilet was about all you were capable of, right? The rest was all up to me. Little me asking strangers for money. Riding my bike to the store. Buying groceries with food stamps. Taking care of the kids you brought into the world."

I jumped out of the chair, paced the floor, and screamed at her as if she were there in the bedroom with me. "You selfish, awful woman! How about when I talked you out of killing yourself? Remember that one? Handing a loaded gun to a twelve-year-old—good job. Were you fucking nuts?"

And then my soul whispered, *In compassion lies divinity.*

Looking back, none of my mother's dysfunction made sense—no one in their right mind would hand a little girl a loaded gun. Could she have suffered from some undiagnosed mental condition that defined the parameters of her life to the four corners of her mattress?

Yes.

I shook off my soul's guidance and screamed primally into a pillow. "I'm still so fucking mad. I took care of you until the day you died, you wretched, disgusting person. And for what? Just to take on all of your responsibility? You left me with nothing except your kid to adopt and your fucking depression. It's twenty years later, and do you know how many days I still lay in bed just like you? Thanks for that. I appreciate you handing down one of your finest attributes. Look at me, here I am a couple of days shy of forty-four years old and—"

I stopped cold.

Mom was forty-four when she died. She was my age. Though I had known this and worried excessively that I, too, might die young, I hadn't focused on what being forty-four meant for her. For me, it was far from the end, or so I hoped, on most days at least. My body was vibrant and strong, my face full and supple. How could it be that everything about her shriveled up and eroded at only the halfway point of existence? Slow, sad tears descended my cheeks. What was it like lying in bed day after day, feeling your body give way to death? Was she scared? Did she want to die? How did it feel when the cancer ate away at her body? Except for Dad, no one really showed her any affection as she lie wasting away.

I gave her what I could—a measured but heartfelt walk toward death, even after the decades of the misery she dealt me. Did impending death entitle her to my full sympathy and affection? I shook off my guilt, remembering how I cleaned her bedsores and swabbed her mouth every day and dripped morphine down her throat every night.

Was that enough?

Did I do enough?

No. Because nothing was ever enough for her.

In the bathroom, I splashed water on my face, hoping it would quell my internal vacillation. I shut off the water and stared in the mirror. Unlike hers, my eyes were green and my hair shades of blonde, but my cheeks and nose, the structural landscape of my face, resembled hers more with every birthday. No matter how hard I tried to forget her, she was there staring back at me every time I looked in the mirror.

Wouldn't it be easier to just forgive her?

Yes.

But how could I possibly after everything she did?

Forgive her, if for no other reason than your own peace.

. . . .

Still carrying the weight of my misery a week later, I tried compassion meditation once again. This time, floating inside my mental landscape, sorrow shook my body. Savage grief tore through me recounting, in no particular order, the beatings, my bloody lips, my throbbing head, visiting Dad in prison. And then my inner little girl appeared in my mind's eye. She pressed her cheek into my belly and sighed. Then she wrapped her energy around me in a warm hug.

"It's time to forgive her."

"You mean Mom? I want to, but I'm scared."

"She's here with us. Do you feel her?"

I did. In my mind's eye she stood before us, fresh faced and beautiful. She radiated a wise spiritual essence.

She said, "It's time to let go of your pain, your anger, all of it. It doesn't serve you."

Over the last few decades, I'd grown accustomed to hating her. There was something strangely rewarding about lugging around all the old pain about what a horrific mother she was. I mean, who would I be if I weren't her victimized, beaten, resentful daughter who spent her life chin-deep in childhood anguish?

What would that look like?

Mom smiled at me, then her full cheeks flushed with wisdom and happiness. Joyful memories of us began to drip between the walls of my resentment. The sun shining on my face while we bebopped around in our convertible singing Motown tunes. Licking my lips, savoring every granule of sweetness in the birthday cakes she bought just for fun. Mom snorting with laughter every time we dipped our forks right down the middle for a bite.

She cradled my cheek in her hand. "I loved you the best I could. It was all part of our work in this lifetime. Our relationship, as painful as it was, was all part of what we're here to learn. And part of that lesson is forgiveness. That is where you'll find peace." Then she opened her arms, inviting me in. "None of it was your fault. You were good and right and full of love. Come. Let me show you."

She opened her arms wider. As I fell into her, her arms turned into wings that wrapped entirely around me.

"Hold tight and feel my energy."

I was a baby in her womb, but quickly her fear and resentment threatened me. I kicked and pushed, trying to keep them away, but before long they seeped through until I was completely submerged in her past.

Her mother walked out and never came back.

Why didn't you love me?

Her father drank away his paychecks.

I'm hungry, Daddy.

Her Ukrainian-speaking grandmother raised her until she died of a heart attack when Mom was twelve.

Why did you leave me all alone, Baba? Who will love me now?

Scrubbing her bloodstained pants after starting her period for the first time.

I'm so ashamed.

Her stepmother beating her.

I'm worthless.

Mom running away from home on her bike and meeting Dad outside his car lot.

He loves me?

He offers her security and safety.

But at what cost? My life?

She's pregnant at nineteen.

I don't know how to be a mother.

Mom opened her arms, and I floated out.

She took my hands and said, "I knew only what I knew. We arrive in the human experience as students. Our work is to fulfill the pacts our souls made with one another. So while it may seem that I didn't love you, I did. I loved you by fulfilling our pact. Know that you were loved. You are loved. You are love."

My body tingled with knowing. My mother might not have been enlightened enough to say this to me when she was alive, but in that moment, I knew it to be the Universe's truth. She kissed me gently on the forehead, sealing my enlightenment. It would take more compassion meditation sessions, journaling, and therapy appointments to release my emotions and process my remaining anger toward her, but

I was ready to do what it took. The emotional release wasn't instant like switching on a light. It felt more like a gradual loosening of a straitjacket.

When we suffer years of trauma and decades of emotional stuffing, our stories bind us so tightly we can barely move beyond their confines. But with each bit of extracting our truth, with each bit of forgiveness, the fabric of the jacket loosens. We experience movement and freedom for the first time ever. And one day, with enough work, the jacket falls to the ground, and we are free to stretch, roam, and run as far as our mind's eye can see.

. . . .

Forgiving Dad came a bit easier than forgiving Mom, but similarly, forgiveness came in phases. The first time I remember feeling compassion for Dad was when we visited him in prison. Sitting across the table from him, there was a glimmer of weakness in his eyes and a broadness to his shoulders. He spent his days working out and churning his legal case over and over in his mind. He didn't want to know much about us except how much money was left and whether Mom was sleeping with other men. There was a caged desperation about him that, sadly, at only twelve years old, I empathized with.

A couple of years later, after he was released from prison, Dad showed up in our driveway one evening unannounced while Mom, my siblings, and I were backing out of the garage. I leapt from the car and wrapped my arms around his waist.

"Dad, I'm so happy you're out," I said, tears of joy and fear alternating down my cheeks.

He glared at Mom and put his arm around me. "Hi, honey."

Dad leaned toward the open car door and said in a sweet tone I didn't know he was capable of, "Hi, kids, did you miss me?"

My sister wailed and my brother screamed, "Mommy!" over and over. I realized that at their young ages and with him having been gone so long, neither of them recognized him. It was hard for anyone to recognize him though; his beard had grown long and scruffy, covering his gaunt face.

"I don't think this is a good idea," Mom said. "You're scaring them." She crossed her arms.

"Do you have any money you can give me?" Dad asked. "All I have are these clothes I was wearing when I went to the joint. I need some money to, you know, start over."

I recognized Dad's blue flannel shirt. I always loved that shirt. It was soft and matched his eyes. And I never remembered seeing lipstick on it.

"I don't have anything for you," Mom said.

"Dad, I'm sorry." I stood near him, tears flowing from my eyes.

From the porch light shining in Dad's face, I could see tears in his eyes, too. I didn't know he knew how to cry.

"Well, I just thought I'd ask." He took a step back. "I'd like to see the kids. Can I?"

"No, I don't think that'd be a good idea," Mom said.

Dad looked at me, disheartened. "Well then, kiddo, I have to go." He tweaked my chin and walked down the driveway and into the dark street.

Where was he going? Had he walked all the way from prison? I watched him walk away until he completely faded into the darkness. I had experienced more than a few heartbreaking moments in my short lifetime. But watching Dad, who was once proud and strong, ask for money with tears in his eyes broke my heart wide open. I would have done anything to hand him the twenty dollars I got from George and Betty.

After Mom died, and with this memory in my mind, I called Dad and told him I forgave him. Well, I didn't actually use those words, but I said that I understood who he was and what he'd been through. It couldn't have been easy to start over with nothing, and yet he forgave Mom. When I hung up, I knew that was likely the last time I'd talk to him. I didn't have any feelings for him—love or hate. I'd finally accepted that he was never going to be the father I wanted or needed, and I had to stop wishing otherwise. Holding contempt for him was doing nothing but reinforcing my story of abandonment. It was time to leave him in the past so I could live fully in the present.

· · · · · · · · · · · · · · · · ·

When you understand what forgiveness really is, it's easier than you think. Forgiveness is never about the other person. It's about you. It's about letting go. It's about choosing yourself over the person who wronged you. Not forgiving someone means you're holding onto the past, to your old stories of victimhood and worthlessness.

Forgiving someone does not mean you must be their friend or have family dinners or even talk to them again. You don't even have to tell them you forgave them! As long as you do it within yourself, that is enough. When considering forgiving others, there are a few truths I'd like you to remember:

You are in charge of your own happiness.

You are the keeper of your energy.

You are the protector of your soul.

These truths will help you let go of ego and the need to be right. You will see that your inner peace and happiness are more important than a grudge. When you forgive those who have wronged you, you are honoring and respecting yourself. It means you are ready to rise above your story.

FORGIVING OURSELVES AND GRIEVING OUR STORY

The final step in extracting our true self and releasing our story is forgiving ourselves for the narratives we wrote and grieving the time we spent living inside them. Once my healing set course, I'd find myself caught up in the inner dialogue of *Why did it take me so long? What did I miss out on during the years it took me to rise above my story?* But this is just *another* story we tell ourselves—that we were wrong, silly, or weak for allowing our story to limit our lives for so long.

The truth is that healing takes as long as it takes. Our story is layered with thin pieces of pain and thicker layers of trauma. Each part must be examined with patience and empathy. For me that meant countless compassion meditation sessions and therapy appointments. It also meant that I would have to finally grieve the original traumas as well as the decades I lost staying entangled in my stories.

My sweet dog Finn initiated this part of my healing because in losing him, the watershed of all my repressed emotions finally opened. Once he died, I couldn't contain my grief. When the walls that kept me scared and emotionally confined eroded, grief roared through me endlessly. Like waves rolling onto shore, some crashing and others gently breaking, my dance with grief was raw and cathartic. That grief flowing through me was one of the first times I felt alive. I'd been living a repressed, unexpressed life, but in the throes of immense sorrow, I knew that to save my life, I had to let it all out. The sadness. The anger. The shame and the rage. I had to grieve not having parents, losing my childhood, and all the years afterward when I lost myself.

Grieving was a long process for me. It would take weeks and sometimes months to pull certain emotions from the depths of me. But what's on the other side of grief is the crispest, brightest light. It's there, waiting to embrace you with warm, loving energy. We are all children of the Divine, and our purpose here is to feel everything we possibly can. That's what being human is—to work through the pain to find the joy. To dive into the darkness to recover the light. Our goal is not to avoid feeling or to shy away from pain. We are here in this life to walk right through the middle of pain and anguish, believing that we are worthy of the beauty on the other side. Every friend, lover, parent, animal, bug, sunray, moonbeam, and rainbow is there to offer us wisdom. We won't ever know pure joy unless we've been swallowed by misery and rescued ourselves from its depths.

Only when you experience the full redemption of grief will you stand in the presence of grace. And that, my beautiful friend, is the key to a meaningful life.

CREATE A FORGIVENESS PRACTICE

As part of my healing journey, I developed a forgiveness practice. I make time each day, even if it's just a few minutes, to forgive myself and others. I include it in my meditation practice, but you can also do it separately.

Begin by sitting or lying comfortably. Close your eyes and inhale and exhale, each for a count of five. When you've established a nice rhythm with your breath, imagine a light moving through your body. The light is warm and healing, and it flows slowly, scanning your body for misunderstanding, grudges, and resentment. Due to the energetic nature of our emotions, you may feel the congested energy in various parts of your body. Let the light flow from your brain to your neck, through your chest and abdomen, down one side of your body and up the other.

If you're still unsure whether you need to forgive yourself or others, ask yourself these questions:

Which negative emotions are you feeling about what happened? Anger? Resentment? Rage? Jealousy?

What's under that top emotion? Fear? Guilt? Shame?

Where do you feel the emotion? In your stomach? Throat? Jaw? If you really tune in, you'll feel it somewhere.

What does that emotion want to say? How can it express itself once and for all? Does it need to laugh, cry, scream, shake, or dance?

Could there be another explanation for what happened? Why the other person acted the way they did?

Can you find compassion?

Do you want to carry around this emotional sludge (I mean this literally, by the way) or release it once and for all?

Honoring your emotions, even the negative ones, is the gateway to forgiveness. If any of these questions resonated with you, give my forgiveness practice a try and tell me that you don't feel lighter, happier, and freer than you've ever felt. Forgiving is a superpower we all have. We just have to tap into it.

LET'S SUM IT UP

This final step before we ultimately rise above is a spiritual and emotional doozy! Here's where we extract our true selves and release our stories. To do this, we must:

1. Rid ourselves of shame.
2. Soothe our inner child.

3. Forgive those who wronged us.

4. Forgive ourselves and grieve our stories.

We can rid ourselves of shame by taking the cloak off our past. Talking openly with someone we trust, such as a spouse, friend, or therapist, is the best way to do this. Soothing our inner child involves processing our old, suppressed emotions and having compassion for what our inner child endured. Forgiving others is a crucial component in the process, but it's easier than you think. Forgiveness is always about you and your inner peace—no one else's. And the best part is those who wronged you don't even have to know you forgave them.

Forgiving ourselves can be a bit more difficult. Sometimes, we get caught up in the woulds and the shoulds and the idea of "wasted time." Trust that there is no such thing. We are here to experience it all, including grief, which is what we'll feel when we're ready to release our old stories. A powerful way to forgive yourself and others is to develop a daily forgiveness practice. It will keep you clean of grudges and resentment.

NOW IT'S YOUR TURN

Extracting your true self and releasing your story is some of the most challenging work we do on this healing journey. It requires brutal honesty and loving compassion in equal measure. This is the time when you examine your pain, which can be the last thing you want to do, but it is the very thing you must do if you are to rise above your story.

Close your eyes and ask that the light of compassion shine through you and empower you to see things as they are and not how they seem. Do your best to turn off your emotional brain and answer these questions with the pure self-awareness of your thinking brain. Here are some prompts to lead you through each step of the process.

RELEASING SHAME:

What are you ashamed of?

How does that shame make you feel?

Have you ever shared the stories of your shame with anyone?

Name one person that you trust enough to share your shame with.

SOOTHING YOUR INNER CHILD:

Do you have a relationship with your inner child?

What are they like? How old are they? What do you call them? How do they feel?

Is there anything your inner child needs to say to you?

What do they need in order to feel happy and loved? Do they need to play? Talk? Be cared for?

If you took your inner child to their favorite place, where would that be?

What would you two do together on the best day you can imagine?

Does your inner child need a hug?

What would make your inner child feel comforted about the past?

FORGIVING OTHERS:

Is there someone you haven't forgiven? Visualize sitting down with them. Try to see things from their perspective. What was their story? Can you find compassion and empathy for them?

What would it take for you to forgive them?

FORGIVING YOURSELF:

Is there something you haven't forgiven yourself for?

Visualize yourself exactly as you were in that moment. Perhaps you were a teenager or a young adult. What did you look like? What were you wearing?

How did you feel? Were you scared? Unsure? Try to see the situation through that version of yourself.

Can you give yourself a hug and find forgiveness?

What does that version of you need to hear?

Is there a loss you haven't yet grieved? What is it? Lost time, loved ones, your childhood, your innocence? What emotion do you need to express or what do you need to say or feel to grieve that loss?

Do something that brings that pain and loss to the surface. Talk to a therapist, listen to fifteen minutes of sad music, write a letter. Try compassion meditation.

Take a few minutes and try the forgiveness practice I explained earlier. Scan your body for stuck energy, grudges, and resentment.

Can you tap into the superpower we call forgiveness?

How does it feel to release some of your old angst? Do you feel lighter or more peaceful?

I'm so proud of you and the truth you've extracted here. I know from experience that it can feel scary and unsettling to have all this pain and discomfort come to the surface. But trust that you are well on your way to rising! Now close your eyes and tell yourself that you are safe, you are loved, and you are worthy of happiness.

9

. . . .

OTHER WAYS TO RELEASE YOUR STORY

f you're still feeling a bit stuck in your limiting stories, don't fret. It's completely normal to still feel tethered to our old ways. Sometimes we need more time and self-examination. Sometimes we need more than traditional therapy. This was certainly true for me. Seeing a therapist did provide relief and clarity, but my wounds were gaping and my stories were still gnarled. I needed more. I wanted to go deeper into my healing.

While our body carries the unresolved energy of our traumas, our soul carries the unresolved karma of our unlearned lessons. As I peeled back the layers of my unresolved trauma, I sensed that there was something luminous, perhaps Divine, inside me waiting to be uncovered. It was my soul. Talk therapy gave me a taste of clean, renewed energy, but I craved mental, physical, and spiritual alignment. Over time, I grew more courageous and inspired to try alternative healing modalities that would unearth my deepest pain.

In the next section, I share a few fascinating tools I used in conjunction with psychotherapy to release my stubborn, age-old stories. I also dive into some interesting modalities that have helped others release their stories as well. These tools are for those seeking physical, mental, and emotional clearing of their trauma. They are also helpful for anyone craving deeper spiritual healing. Everyone's journey is unique, and this is the perfect time to experiment and do what feels right for you. As with trying any new healing modality, it's always best to consult your doctor beforehand.

HOLOTROPIC BREATHWORK

Our breathing is the link between the physical world and the soul.
—Wim Hof

"What are you looking to release?" the spiritual guide asked me.

"I've had an overwhelming fear of abandonment for as long as I can remember."

She scribbled in her notebook. "And?"

I wanted to say, *And my dog's dying and it's almost the twentieth anniversary of my mom dying, who by the way, I never grieved and still hate to this day.* But the words halted on my lips as all the memories of my abusive, neglectful mother percolated thick and heavy in my mind.

Instead, I rubbed my furrowed brow and said, "That's pretty much it."

She peered at me over her glasses for a long few seconds before dimming the lights and reclining my chair. She covered me with one of those fuzzy blankets from Oprah's Favorite Things list circa 2004 and told me to close my eyes and breathe quickly.

Breathwork has been practiced for centuries to create altered states of consciousness. Holotropic (a word of Greek origin that means "moving toward wholeness") breathwork was developed in the 1970s by psychiatrists Stanislav and Christina Grof.[44] This type of deep, fast breathing can heal past trauma by uncovering repressed memories and subconscious emotional patterns. With their trademarked breathing technique, the Grofs forged a spiritual gateway to subconscious healing that's offered many people reprieve without the use of mind-altering drugs.

Ever the trier of anything promising wholeness, wellness, spiritual awakening, or regular bowel movements, I absolutely had to try Holotropic breathwork. It might not solve my frequent constipation, but there were other things stuck in me that I knew had to be released.

I closed my eyes and breathed short, staccato breaths. *In. Out. In. Out. Quicker. Shorter.* With each breath, memories clicked on and off like a camera shutter.

The guide's voice brought me back to the room. "I will check in with you every minute or so while you're breathing and your memories are churning. Most memories will come and go quickly. When one sticks, tell me. Stay with the quick breaths even when it gets physically uncomfortable, and it will. The only way out is through."

My memories slowed a bit as if I were flipping through the pages of a book. The smell of Mom's bedsores. My yellow rain boots. Holding my husband's hand. Whoopsie's tear-stained fur. Dad's garage. Bondo under my fingernails. Finn's face. George and Betty. My green-and-white bike. Kissing Will, my best friend from law school, in his parents' basement.

In.

Out.

In.

Out.

The ocean.

The ocean.

I gasped.

"Keep breathing," she said. "Are you somewhere you can't look away from? Stay right there. That's our work," she said softly.

I flinched. Then moaned.

My stomach tightened like a clamshell, coaxing me to curl forward and close myself off from the memory.

"I'm here with you," she said. "Talk to me. Where are you?"

"A beach. I've never been here before."

"Who do you see?"

A man. His dark, curly hair was long and unkempt. His body was frail and dark with sun. I didn't recognize him as anyone I knew in this life, but looking in his eyes, his spirit was familiar. And from the weight of my heart, I knew exactly who he was.

"My lover."

"What's happening?"

"We're on the beach, and . . ."

"And what?"

"Don't go!" A wave of panic flooded through me.

"Breathe and tell me what's happening."

"He's leaving! He's leaving me!"

My lover kissed me on the forehead and walked backward away from me.

"I love you," he said. "I'll always love you." And then he turned and walked calmly into the ocean.

"Don't go! Come back!" I yelled over and over.

My body was in the dark, cold room with the spiritual guide but my soul was kneeling on the hot sand. Salty tears stung my sunburned cheeks.

"Don't leave me here. Don't leave me alone." I watched him swim far off into the distance and disappear below the waves, succumbing to death. I cried and shook with grief until I felt his spirit radiating above me. Then he passed into Universal light.

"Look down at your body and tell me what you look like," the healer said.

"My feet are dirty and my body is emaciated. My hair is long, to my waist."

"Why do you look like that?"

"I've been on this island a long time. And now I'm alone. He was sick. He left me—alone."

"Were you deserted?"

"Yes. In an accident. We were there together for years. But no one came for us."

"What happened next?"

"I walked the island each day patching together pieces of stories I remembered reading in books. And at night, I slept on a mat of woven palm fronds. I covered myself with the only remnant of our belongings—a once colorful blanket that was now tattered and worn."

"How long did you stay on that island?"

"For the rest of my life."

"Alone?"

"Yes."

"When does that life end for you?"

"Years later. No one comes for me, and the loneliness is too much. I eat a handful of poisonous berries and wrap myself in my cherished blanket. I stare into the bright sky, feeling the sun warm my body until—"

"Until what?" she asked.

"My spirit . . ."

My breathing resumed its normal rhythm, and I opened my eyes. I was exhausted. The healer turned up the lights and sat back in her chair.

"Have you ever had a past-life regression?" she asked.

"No."

"They don't always happen in breathwork, but they can if your soul needs to release an old wound."

What she said felt right to me.

"What was your takeaway? As your spirit floated above your body, how did you feel?"

"Eternally wounded. The loss was too much to bear."

"Sometimes our souls get stuck with karmic baggage on their way out; they take something with them that they should've left behind. And if they carry it with them into another life, the lesson repeats. You must let go of your fear of abandonment or you will face it again and again."

The chill rolling through my body told me she was right. Perhaps I chose this life with all its abandonment so I could finally let go of my fear of being alone, so I could finally know that I was enough. Would I face loss after loss until I trusted that I would be okay no matter what happened? Was this the spiritual lesson I was here to learn?

"How do I let it go?"

"Look around you. The opportunity is always there. You may not like the form it's in, but the Universe *always* gives you the opportunity."

As I drove home, the external world appeared brighter. Colors were more saturated. The air was rich and lush. My body felt purposeful and engaged. But my inner landscape—that's where I felt the most freedom. I felt lighter and not so tightly bound.

While past life regressions like mine are not guaranteed in Holotropic breathwork, what can be expected is a greater awareness of yourself and your story. It assists in the release of your story because in that altered consciousness you see that there's a deeper reason for the pain you carry. You also unlock the limiting subconscious patterns of the emotional brain by releasing repressed memories and emotions. I found that Holotropic breathwork reduced my anxiety and leveled my mood. I also sensed there was a greater purpose for my pain. We'll dive more into this idea in the next chapter.

I was not healed after my first experience with Holotropic breathwork, but I did go back for more sessions. In fact, I still do! Breathwork opened me up to the idea that there is not one direct path to wholeness. The Universe offers a plethora of options for us to release our stories and find peace. We just have to be willing to try them. As this practice involves voluntary hyperventilation, Holotropic breathwork should be practiced with a certified instructor who will lead you safely through the two-to-three-hour session.

COLD THERAPY

As we've learned, the autonomic nervous system (triggered by the emotional brain) runs our fight-or-flight response. When this stress response gets stuck in overdrive, we feel anxious, depressed, disassociated, withdrawn, and exhausted. Historically we thought it impossible to voluntarily influence this part of our nervous system, meaning we believed we couldn't change the automatic functions of our body.

A cold therapy guru named Wim Hof has proven otherwise.[45]

While cold showers have been a part of our lives and vocabulary for years, Hof has developed a particular method of cold exposure, breathing exercises, and meditation that he calls the Wim Hof Method (WHM). Through numerous scientific studies, he's shown that the nervous and immune systems can be voluntarily influenced by exposure to cold, meaning it is possible to shift yourself out of fight, flight, or freeze with cold water therapy. This includes cold showers, standing in a barrel of icy water, or, if you're like Wim, cannonballing into a freezing lake.

The science behind cold exposure espouses that because it's momentarily stressful to the body, your brain releases endorphins, the feel-good and happy hormones, thus making a mood boost a pretty certain result. It also claims that repeated everyday stressors like cold exposure train the body and the nervous system to fluctuate and then regulate. In other words, just like lifting weights trains your muscles, cold therapy trains the nervous system. Remember, a resilient nervous system is a healthy nervous system! WHM fans have touted improvement of autoimmune disorders, depression, anxiety, bipolar disorder, and more.

Because I'm a lover of sun and heat, I resisted cold therapy for years. Just the idea of a cold shower made me shudder. But as I've learned, if you want to heal, you must walk right through the pain and discomfort. The only way out is through. And so, I tried the WHM. And while you can just take the shower or the bath, I found the added WHM components of controlled breathing and meditation added much more to the experience. After practicing the WHM, I felt alive and energized. My mood shifted upward, and I discovered a new calm that enabled me to handle stressful situations with more patience. The WHM also gave me a deep sense of empowerment and resilience knowing that I could find ease in the face of discomfort. Your cold shower awaits, my friends!

MEDITATION

As I mentioned earlier, I learned to meditate after my colossal breakup with Jack. And let me just say that it was outrageously uncomfortable at first. There I was, sitting alone, with nothing but my thoughts when I wasn't supposed to be thinking at all. The more thoughts I had, the more I felt like a failure. But here's the thing: Meditation is a *practice*. You aren't supposed to be good at it at first, and the majority of us won't ever have a session without a thought dancing through our minds. I mean, we're not Buddha, and that's okay.

Meditation is and always will be a game changer. Why? It is a powerful way to practice mindfulness, or presence in the moment, and to stay consciously aware of our thoughts, emotions, and physical being. And by now we know that elevating our thoughts and being to a higher level of consciousness is key for healing. Being mindful in meditation nurtures our self-awareness, eventually shedding light on the stories we tell ourselves.

Meditation is also how we reconnect to ourselves, to our souls, and to the Universe. It's where we use our breath as a gateway to something higher. It's also how we become an observer. This is so crucial in rising above our stories. When we become an observer, we see life happening around us, not *to* us. When we meditate, we disengage from our pain and see the thoughts and memories that pop up through an objective lens instead of a subjective one.

In addition, meditation has many health benefits, such as improving sleep quality and reducing your resting heart rate and blood pressure.[46] Research has also shown that meditation may help relieve symptoms of anxiety and depression.[47] For those of us who are still feeling the physical and emotional effects of trauma, meditation's benefits can prove to be quite remarkable.

There are countless forms of meditation. You already know about compassion meditation from chapter 8, which helped me soothe my inner child and forgive my mother. You can also visualize your breath or a color, or you can imagine that you're lying on a beach in Bali. You can visualize scanning your body with colorful light or repeat a calming word or mantra. There are also a variety of meditation apps available, such as Headspace, Calm, and Insight Timer, if you want more structured guidance. Whatever form works for you, do it. There is no right or wrong way to meditate. You simply have to rest comfortably, close your eyes, and breathe.

INFRARED SAUNA

I've been using saunas for years. There was something about the heat that soothed the deepest parts of me long before I learned about its health benefits. (My love of the warmth also explains why I moved from the blustery Midwest to sunny Florida.)

I began using traditional saunas at hotels when I traveled. I discovered that a hearty sweat brought me back to life after a long flight or a bit of overindulgence. About ten years ago, I was introduced to infrared saunas as a way to help my stress and anxiety levels. By the end of my first session, I was hooked. Besides soaked and sweaty, I left relaxed, happy, and emotionally five pounds lighter. Ever curious about how and why things work, I looked deeper into infrared therapy, and here's what I discovered.

While traditional saunas heat the air, which in turn heats the body, infrared saunas use light to heat the body.[48] This results in a greater detoxification of the organs without the high temperatures of a traditional sauna. Maximum health benefits can be achieved with an infrared thermostat set between 110 and 135 degrees Fahrenheit.

In addition to detoxification, infrared saunas offer other health benefits, such as improved immune function and increased blood circulation. And for those of us with unresolved trauma, anxiety, or depression, infrared saunas may also increase our feel-good hormones like dopamine, norepinephrine, and serotonin, while decreasing cortisol, our stress hormone, thus leaving us feeling happier and more relaxed. The therapeutic effect of heat on the body and the mind is, without question, profound. In fact, a 2018 study showed that sauna use is a resoundingly successful treatment for various mental disorders.[49]

After years of getting my infrared fix at spas, I invested in my own infrared sauna and now get my dose of feel-good heat two to three times a week in the comfort of my own home. Sometimes I use it along with cold therapy, rotating between the sauna and cold showers every twenty to thirty minutes. I also use my time in the sauna to meditate or check in with my inner child. Now there's some healthy multitasking!

EMOTIONAL FREEDOM TECHNIQUE OR TAPPING

The Emotional Freedom Technique, or tapping, is a powerful tool we can use on a daily basis to release negative thoughts and emotions from the body. Tapping is based on the body's energy meridian system as described in Chinese medicine. It's similar in concept to acupuncture but without the use of needles. Instead, you use your fingertips to tap five to seven times on nine meridian points of the body while focusing on and speaking about the emotion you're feeling. By acknowledging your emotion (self-awareness is always the first step in healing!) while tapping on the meridians, you release the physical energy associated with the emotion.[50] Sounds pretty powerful, right? Here's how we do it.

Identify the meridian points you will tap in this order:

1. The side of the hand (think karate chop zone!).
2. The beginning of the eyebrow.
3. The side of the eye.
4. Under the eye.
5. Under the nose.
6. The chin (more specifically, the crease between lip and chin).
7. The collarbone.
8. The underarm (a hand's width below your armpit).
9. The top of the head.

Next, create your "set-up statement" in which you identify and acknowledge the emotion you're feeling. Maybe it's anger, anxiety, or fear. Then, add a positive affirmation of acceptance. Putting it all together, you might say something like this:

Even though I have this anxiety, I love and accept myself.

Now, tap the side of your hand (karate chop zone) while saying your statement three times.

Then as you tap the other meridian points five to seven times each, speak freely about how you're feeling. While tapping, you might say something like:

I'm just so overwhelmed. I don't know if I can do all this. There's so much on my plate right now, and I can't make everyone happy. There's never any time for myself. I just run around checking boxes. I feel like a robot.

The gift of tapping is that it allows for the space and time to acknowledge how you're feeling. Instead of suppressing or ignoring our emotions, we bring them out into the light of day until their hold over us is no more. It's amazing how wonderful tapping can make you feel.

That's why an estimated ten million people have used tapping to alleviate trauma symptoms such as anxiety and depression. In fact, it has been used extensively to treat war veterans with PTSD as well as survivors of the Rwandan Genocide.[51]

I use tapping on an almost daily basis, whether to work through an old emotion that suddenly resurfaces or to clear away current disappointment, impatience, or anger. I simply find a private, quiet space and tap away at the negative emotions clouding my day. It's a quick and easy way to soothe yourself in the midst of chaos or help release old vestiges of your story.

YOGA

Yoga is one of my favorite ways to dislodge a stuck story. For thousands of years, yoga has offered a way to transcend our physical bodies and connect with our souls. Unlike what we see today—bodies taking shape in down dog or side crow—yoga wasn't born of physical movement.

That came later. Its original purpose was to shift us inward to the soul and find the answers we most seek using meditation.

A 2014 study conducted by Dr. Bessel van der Kolk and supported by the National Institutes of Health found that ten weeks of consistent yoga practice significantly reduced the participants' PTSD symptoms.[52] An interesting note to the study is that these same patients had previously tried medication to relieve their symptoms to no avail.

I fell in love with yoga circa 2005 after Jack fell out of love with me. After too many happy hours that weren't so happy, a friend suggested that we ditch the wine and instead go to a Bikram yoga class. I reluctantly agreed, but the second I walked into that 105-degree room I was hooked. (My love of heat is real, y'all!) Over the next ninety minutes, we did two breathing exercises and twenty-four postures (most performed twice). Between the heat and the asanas, I was so consumed that I couldn't think about anything else, including my ex-lover. I left the studio euphoric.

My love affair with yoga evolved over the years as I tried every type I could: heated vinyasa, yoga nidra, Ashtanga, yin, and restorative. I learned to listen to my body and give it what it needed. It was no longer about hot and grueling. I didn't always want to punish myself just to get a high. I wanted to be good to my body. But more importantly, I wanted to feel good in my soul. As yoga fed my desire to resolve the happenings of my life, it also invited me to discover the treasures I had buried inside me.

With its nonjudgmental nature, yoga welcomed and soothed me. I felt secure on the mat beneath my feet and between the four walls that embraced me. With time and trust, yoga offered me countless emotional releases. A heart-opener like camel pose always does me in. It's okay, though. I'm not the only one crying after doing a backbend and shining my heart to the sky. I'm never sorry for rolling out my mat because, as I've learned in rising above my story, showing up for yourself is the only way the work gets done.

EMDR

Eye movement desensitization and reprocessing (EMDR) is a widely studied technique shown not only to lessen symptoms of PTSD but, in some cases, heal them after just several treatments.[53]

EMDR was developed in 1990 by Dr. Francine Shapiro, who theorized that after a traumatic event, the memory of the trauma and the resulting negative emotions get stuck, unprocessed in the emotional brain. We know this to be true when, as we learned, during and after a traumatic event, the emotional brain hoards information and fails to send it to the thinking brain for processing. A blockage results in the emotional brain, which replays the memory repeatedly, causing distress to the nervous system, also known as fight, flight, or freeze overdrive.

Most EMDR treatments involve some form of bilateral brain stimulation, or the use of both the left and right sides of the brain, to integrate and process the memory. The patient follows a visual stimulus, such as the practitioner moving their finger back and forth, while thinking about the traumatic memory. Some treatments may include alternating tones or taps.[54] The goal is to unblock the negative emotion surrounding the memory and transform it into a positive one. For instance, EMDR may change a feeling of powerlessness into power or one of shame into self-love. In this process, a mental shift occurs from the emotional brain to the thinking brain, relieving the emotional distress.

Recalling the traumatic memory may cause a fight-or-flight response, sweating, or increased heart rate. Therefore, it's recommended that you receive EMDR treatment from a trained therapist.

VAGAL NERVE STIMULATION

The vagus nerve is actually a nerve network that runs from your brain to your large intestine.[55] Also known as the "information superhighway" of the body, it plays a huge part in regulating our heart rhythm, swallowing, breathing, and digestion.[56] We know by now that the autonomic nervous system is made up of the sympathetic and parasympathetic nervous systems. We also know that the sympathetic (along with the emotional brain) is what triggers the fight-or-flight response. But when the threat has passed, it's the vagus nerve, as part of the parasympathetic system, that calms us down.[57] If the vagus nerve doesn't do its job effectively, our sympathetic nervous system can get stuck in fight or flight.

Research suggests that vagal nerve stimulation can reduce PTSD symptoms by reducing specific inflammation in the body as well as counteracting the fight-or-flight response.[58] While researchers and therapists use different devices and modalities to activate the nerve,[59] there are ways we can activate the vagus nerve on our own, including:

- singing, chanting, or humming
- gargling
- massaging your throat
- cold therapy (which helps build resilience in the nervous system)
- meditation and yoga (which help regulate the nervous system)

I also like to throw in some like-you-mean-it hugging to stimulate my vagus nerve because, as it turns out, vagal nerve stimulation also helps release the love hormone oxytocin (which is also released during sex), making us feel more connected to others. A well-tuned vagus nerve goes a long way in helping us find peace after a stressful situation, so get to singing and hugging. It will do your mind and your body good.

SOMATIC THERAPY

Based on the idea that trauma can become trapped in the body as well as the brain, Somatic Experiencing (SE) may help release that energy.[60] SE can be especially beneficial for those who are experiencing dysregulation, or stress response overdrive. Created by Dr. Jack Levine in the 1970s, SE has been effective in alleviating symptoms of PTSD.[61] Levine's theory of healing came from watching wild animals, who, after being chased by predators, shook, trembled, ran, or had some type of energetic release after their fight-or-flight response was triggered. Once the physical release occurred, the animal's stress response returned to normal.

Seeking a similar, well-regulated response in humans, SE uses physical touch, meditation, breathing exercises, dancing, and other techniques to release the stored energy, thus resetting the physical aspects of the trauma response.

There are over twelve thousand professionals trained in somatic therapy. And while no two sessions are the same, what you can expect is a gentle revisiting of the traumatic event and the circumstances surrounding it. Like other healing modalities that require a dip into the past, be prepared for a possible trigger. If somatic therapy is something you'd like to explore, find a trained therapist with whom you connect and feel safe.

HYPNOSIS

Hypnosis was a powerful part of my healing journey. Guided by a trusted and trained therapist, I used hypnotherapy to re-examine traumatic moments of my childhood. Through various relaxation and recall techniques, the therapist helped me reframe the memories surrounding my trauma. Hypnosis can also help retrain your self-talk from negative to positive.[62] After my sessions, I was flooded with joy. Day by day, I felt more positive and upbeat. In addition to reframing traumatic memories and changing negative thought patterns, hypnosis has also been found to significantly alleviate symptoms of depression.[63]

RHYTHM THERAPY

We're born with a penchant for rhythm. In fact, we first develop our rhythmic vibe in the womb. Our mother walking or talking as well as her heartbeat and breathing set the earliest cadence of our life.[64] Once we arrive into the bright lights of the world, it's the rocking, swaying, and bouncing that soothes the emotional brain.

If we experience early childhood trauma and don't receive this rhythmic soothing from our parents or caretakers, our stress response becomes dysregulated. And as we know, unresolved childhood trauma can cause our stress response to stay in overdrive well into adulthood. Renowned trauma researchers and doctors Bruce Perry[65] and Bessel van der Kolk[66] promote the use of rhythm therapy to help heal trauma. In addition to helping with self-regulation, rhythm therapy can also help with co-regulation by making us feel connected to others and the rhythmic nature of the world.[67]

Rhythm therapy can be part of professional treatment, but it can also become part of your daily routine. There are more than a few ways you can experience the benefits of rhythm: singing, dancing, running, swimming, skiing, sailing, and drumming. I often find these rhythmic activities make me happier. Without a doubt, they soothe the anxious or withdrawn part of me. These activities also connect me to the harmonious frequency of the Universe. Such a connection might also stir up a spiritual knowing that there's more out there for us than pain and limitation. I dare you to tell me you don't feel joyous and free when you shake your booty or bang on a drum.

THE LOVE OF ANIMALS

I believe we're all spiritually connected and that a grand part of our journey here on Earth is to learn from each other—both people and animals. Anyone who's loved an animal knows that these furry souls will teach you what you need to know most. For some of us it's patience, tuning in, or being in the moment. For others, it's something even more powerful, more life-altering, more spiritual. That's what happened to me.

You know about my Finn, the ginger-haired golden retriever whose love positioned me to finally rise above my story. The first time I hoisted him high over my head and our eyes met, I knew he was going to change me. I just had no idea how much. He started shifting me subtly. Laying on me when I felt anxious. Coaxing me for a walk when I paced the kitchen. It was as if his soul was whispering, *Relax, Mom. Smile, Mom.*

As months turned into years, even with all his goofy tendencies, Finn flourished into my spiritual guide. With each lick to my face and gentle sigh into my ear, I felt unconditionally loved for the first time in my life. And as he eased me into his warm security, I thought about all the trauma and unresolved emotions I'd been carrying around with me for decades.

When I clutched that deep pain with all of my might, terrified to let it out, Finn spiritually doubled down. At seven years old, he was diagnosed with an aggressive form of cancer that the doctors said was incurable. I couldn't bear the thought of losing the only being that had ever unconditionally loved me, and my story of abandonment once again took over my life.

Although my sweet boy didn't survive his cancer, his life was nothing short of miraculous, because in losing him, in watching his spirit float toward the heavens, the watershed of my grief finally opened. He knew that if he left me, I couldn't contain my grief. If I were going to save my life, I had to finally grieve the deepest losses and trauma still festering inside me.

I had a lot more healing to do well after Finn died, but losing him was the impetus to me finally releasing my story. When I had to lose someone I loved so much in order to become whole, I released my story of abandonment. It's such a beautifully perfect irony to heal yourself with the very situation that caused the pain in the first place. Animals are the windows to our souls, and they're here to help make us whole. They help us see what we need most, and they are often our very best teachers.

And just in case the unconditional love isn't enough to sway you to get a dog, studies have shown that dogs relieve symptoms of anxiety and depression.[68] Playing with and loving dogs causes an increase in oxytocin levels (also known as the love hormone).[69] This happy hormone causes us to feel connected to and in tune with others, including those without fur.

LSD AND PSILOCYBIN

Many people have used psychedelic drugs such as LSD and psilocy-bin, a hallucinogenic chemical found in more than one hundred types of mushrooms, to heal unresolved trauma.[70] I have not. I don't hold judg-ment about their use and have learned from others the potential benefits of using these drugs in the presence of a guide. Psychedelics are gaining popularity in trauma therapy and are therefore worth mentioning here. I leave it to you to do your own research and look inward for guidance on whether using psychedelics feels right for you.

. . . .

LET'S SUM IT UP

While traditional talk therapy has its place and value, healing on a pro-found level requires a holistic approach, one that uncovers even the deepest, most entangled emotions and stories. Some of the alternative modalities available to us have hundreds if not thousands of years of backing, while others are on the modern end of the healing spectrum. If you're looking for deeper, whole-picture healing, I encourage you to explore these options and see what feels right for you. They just might be good for your mind, body, *and* soul.

NOW IT'S YOUR TURN

Which of these healing modalities intrigued you the most and why?

Which ones are you willing to try?

What steps can you take to try the ones that interest you most?

This was powerful work we did here in part 2. Kudos! You now understand how you got tangled up in your story and how your story took over your life. Again, self-awareness is the key to your healing. We learned how to extract our true selves. I also shared some alternative methods for dislodging your story and finding deeper spiritual healing. With all this newfound knowledge, you're ready to take the final steps in rising above your story. We're almost there! Let's keep going.

Part 3

. . . .

RISING ABOVE THE STORY

When the rain washes you clean, you'll know.
—Stevie Nicks

. . . .

10

HOW YOUR STORY CAN SERVE YOU—FINDING THE SILVER LINING

Congratulations! You've made it to the final steps in rising above your story. While the end of our healing expedition is in sight, there is still important work to do before we ultimately rise above. This, my friends, is where our journey blossoms! We're going to explore how our stories (and their underlying trauma) can serve us by finding their silver lining.

For a long time, we've been servants to our stories. We've allowed their dark, insidious nature to control our lives. But what if we flipped the script on our stories? What if we asked ourselves how they can serve us? I know it might seem counterintuitive to think that something that caused us so much pain could actually be a blessing, but let's dig in with a heart full of love and find the silver lining in our story.

I know from my own journey that finding a silver lining after trauma is tough, and it can feel impossible. But after everything you've accomplished so far, I have no doubt that you can do this, too. You're so close to finally rising above your story—you can't stop now.

Just to get your gears turning on this oh-so-important piece of the puzzle, here's a peek into how I ultimately uncovered the silver lining in my abandonment and parentification stories.

. . . .

The late winter snow was gray and dirty the morning Mom went in for her scheduled C-section. She made me skip school so I could be there for my brother Brandon's arrival. I would've rather been in my eighth-grade homeroom having Danny Snyder call me "Cabbage Patch kid" than at the hospital with Ed, Brandon's father. It wasn't so much Ed's ratty jean jacket, his diamond chip earrings, or even his mullet that fueled my disdain for him. It was his chain-smoking that drove me bonkers. Even when his newborn son was set to make his grand debut, he'd step outside every few minutes for a cigarette. When he'd come back in, the odor of his smoke-infested clothes made my stomach turn. Part of me wished he'd go out for a smoke and never come back.

"Hey, Ed, how was your eighty-seventh smoke break?" I asked.

"Why do you have to be like that?" He shot me a nasty glance.

"Like what?"

"A sarcastic bitch like your mother."

"Listen here, Ed. I am nothing like my mother. First of all, I'd never get knocked up by a guy like you. And second of all—"

He laughed. "You don't even care that I called your mother a bitch?"

"I've heard worse, Ed."

"I'm sure you have, kid."

Ed was nowhere to be found when a nurse came in the waiting room to give us the news. She was plump and jolly, her bleach-blonde hair pulled back with a bright pink scrunchie.

"Hip hip hooray! It's your lucky day. Your baby brother is finally here," she said with a guffaw.

"Great," I said, not at all trying to hide my apathy.

"Come on, honey. What kind of excitement is that?" Her smile was big and cheeky and slightly nauseating. "Where's your dad?"

"He just got out of prison, but my mom won't let me see him. She spent all his money, so you know . . . it's kinda weird."

Her eyes were now as wide as her smile.

"Well then, let's go see your baby brother." She grabbed my hand, her clammy palm enveloping mine.

"I know where the nursery is." I pulled my hand away and raced off ahead of her.

I traced my finger along the glass while scanning the nursery's sea of blue blankets. *He's probably the ugly one with a mullet*, I thought, imagining Ed squished down to baby size.

And then I spotted him. Without even looking at the name card, I knew it was him. My apathy evaporated. He was perfect and beautiful and familiar to me, as if we'd known each other forever. But even more than that, I knew Mom wasn't capable of giving him what he needed, and neither was his tobacco-toking father. In this lifetime, I knew I was destined to be more than just his sister. I put my palm on the glass, outstretched my fingers, and made him an oath.

"There'll be a lot of sad times coming your way, little one. For that, I'm sorry. It's just the way it is. But I have fourteen years of experience under my belt, and I promise to love and protect you the best I can."

Then I went to find Ed and prayed the doctor had tied Mom's tubes.

A few months later, my wish about Ed came true: he went out for a smoke and didn't come back. While Brandon and I had two siblings between us in age, he and I shared a connection, a spiritual familiarity, that bound us tightly together. Every day after school, I'd scoop him up and take him to my room, where I'd tell him all about my hideously lonely day. He'd listen and smile and sometimes throw his slobbery toy on the floor, which I imagined was his way of saying, "That sucks!" He'd look at me with pure love and adoration. No one had looked at me like that since my puppy Whoopsie.

Our connection grew even stronger on that fateful January afternoon nine years later when the paramedics hoisted Mom's dead body onto the gurney. I knew, as sure as the sky was blue, that the gods of karma were coming for me. I'd promised Brandon that I'd protect him, and now it was time to pay up. With Ed long out of the picture, there was no one to raise him but me.

As her emaciated body floated past me, the stench of her bedsores filled my nostrils. My mind swirled in disbelief. She'd been sick for so long, yet there was something about her stubbornness and sarcasm that convinced me she might live forever. The hospice nurse wrapped her arms around me when my head spun with dizziness.

"I know," she said, steadying my stagger. "It's a lot to take in."

The two feet poking out from under the dining room table ultimately stabilized me. Brandon was hiding there—the parade of the passing too much for him to witness. I crawled under the table and met him. His face was sweaty and streaked with tears, so I pulled him into me and rocked him gently.

"I know. It's scary, huh?" I whispered.

"Uh huh," he cried. "And we won't ever see her again?"

"No. But I'm here."

"Can we stay here for awhile? I'm scared to go out there," he said, squeezing me even tighter.

"As long as you want," I said. The truth was I didn't want to face our situation either.

We stayed intertwined until the paramedics closed the front door. All we had left was a house filled with the winter's bleak air and each other. I was twenty-four going on forty, but there was nothing in my arsenal of experience that told me the right thing to do for a nine-year-old boy who'd just lost his mother. I decided on dinner at his favorite Mexican restaurant. My brother would soon become my adopted son, but before we assumed our new roles, I needed to just be a girl drinking a beer.

As much as I loved Brandon, motherhood was not a role I wanted. After years of mothering my mother and my three siblings, my bio-logical urge to procreate had officially died along with her. But now, I was going to be a mother whether I wanted to or not. I resented her for leaving me to raise Brandon as much as I resented giving up my childhood. Not having been mothered myself, I was also terrified that I didn't have the tools to nurture this boy who deserved more than the life he was dealt.

Within months of Mom's death, Ed returned from his nine-year smoke break and challenged my request to adopt Brandon. For years he'd refused to pay child support and declined all offers to visit his son. Other than his thick, curly hair, there was little connection between

Brandon and this man who did nothing but deposit sperm, eat our food, and abandon us.

There were parts of me that struggled incessantly with the enormity of raising Brandon and what I'd have to sacrifice—my twenties, my thirties . . . my freedom. Now *that* was the real zinger. Up to that point in my life, I'd never experienced true freedom. I'd never lived alone. I was always in charge. The responsible one. I never got to act my age. To have fun. To be carefree.

And in those days of yet another life upheaval, I knew I was meant to save Brandon. I couldn't bear to give him away, let alone to someone who'd abandoned him years before. If I did, I'd be no better than Ed or Mom, or Mom's mother and father, all of whom abandoned their children. I didn't want Brandon to feel the pain of being unloved and orphaned any more than he already did. By adopting him, by choosing him, by standing up in court and fighting for him, could I break our familial pattern of abandonment? My wounds of abandonment were deep and raw, even more so than I was willing to acknowledge at the time, but I wanted to change what I could, to do what I could, to make Brandon's life better. So, there, on the cusp of losing the only child I would ever have (and in spite of my story), my maternal instincts rose from the dead and I waged a legal war to keep him safe.

The judge granted my petition to adopt Brandon. Having a seventy-year-old man legally proclaim me Brandon's mother didn't give me the confidence I needed for the role, but it was a start. Love and patience would have to do the rest.

Brandon was afraid of the dark for the first few years we were together as mother and son. He'd often ask me to lie down with him in bed until he fell asleep. I'd like to say I did it unselfishly. But the truth was I needed to hold onto him, too. Just like when we hid under that dining room table on the day Mom died, clinging to each other. We both needed a life preserver.

As I lay in bed with him on those nights, listening to his dreamy mumbling, I thought about how I would raise him. I wanted him to have a childhood—as normal as possible—with friends and sports and video games. But I also wanted him to be mature and independent. If something happened to me as it did to our mother, I wanted him to be able to take care of himself. I formulated a risk management plan to make Brandon as independent as possible.

By age eleven, he was well-versed in the art of separating colors from whites and making the perfect grilled cheese sandwich. I'd married Max by then, and while I worked long hours as a new lawyer and Max was focused on his business, Brandon taught his friends how to iron and helped their moms carry in groceries.

As this sweet boy metamorphosed into a kind and thoughtful young man, he paused just long enough to learn how to shave, drive a car, land his first job, kiss a few girls, and write for the school newspaper. In the midst of our busy lives, we'd find joyous moments, rolling down the car windows and singing along to "How Bizarre" by OMC. Ours wasn't a traditional family, but after a few years, I began to feel like a real mother.

When Brandon went to college, I was lost. For years, I'd dreamt of the day I'd be alone and have no day-to-day responsibility for him. But being without him deflated me. I was now freshly divorced from Max and an empty nester at only thirty-two years old. This is where we insert my near self-annihilation after my breakup with Jack. And, as you know, my story of abandonment roared wildly once again, as anxiety and panic fueled my every step.

My relationship with Brandon evolved quickly in the four years he was in college. He no longer needed my motherly attention. Much to my dismay, he was as self-sufficient as I had taught him to be. He made his own money, did his own laundry, and cooked his own meals. He came home less often because the life he so skillfully created for himself kept him happily occupied.

Our phone conversations began to take more of a sibling tone as he shared his escapades with me. He called me the day after he met a pretty girl at a party and told me about his plans to take her on a date. After his return from a semester in Europe, he was worldly and carefree. My brother no longer needed me to be his mother.

We'd come so far. We were no longer those poor, struggling kids hiding under the dining room table. He wasn't that little boy singing along to my music. He was singing his own music, on his own time, in his own city. For every second I had resented becoming his mother at twenty-four years old, I was now filled with gratitude—adopting him was my chance to be a mother.

While raising him wasn't easy, and I certainly wasn't perfect, being my brother's mother turned out to be one of my greatest blessings. I discovered that I had deep fortitude and endless grace and that even though I hadn't been mothered, I still possessed an eternal geyser of love. It would take me another decade to fully unearth and heal my stories of abandonment and parentification. But my relationship with Brandon steadily chipped away at my stories, subtly reinforcing my place in the world not just as his mother but as a person worthy of laughter, friendship, and love.

Now that's a silver lining!

FINDING THE SILVER LINING

If we look deep enough, there's always something that makes us stronger, wiser, more insightful, or more compassionate from the pain we endure. Perhaps, like me, you'll find that your life may even feel more complete because of what you went through. Maybe you met someone uplifting, changed careers, or moved to a new city because of your pain. And all in all, while the story and its false underpinnings are hurting you, the positive shift in your physical landscape is tangible. That is what we call a bright spot in a dark sky. It's the silver lining. Grab onto it as we sail toward the finish line.

In addition to the palpable ways in which you can let your story serve you, there can also be positive energetic shifts that occur inside us. We discover a piece of ourselves we hadn't noticed before. In times of friction, we may discover we have boundless grace. In the darkest spiritual winters, we unearth our inner fortitude. We're able to now sense the lushness of the world in the midst of a barren emotional landscape. Undoubtedly, our trauma leaves its imprint, but we can have the story surrounding it serve us by creating a fuller, richer life. In doing so, we let go of could've and should've, and instead we see that we are exactly where we're meant to be.

Another beautiful way to have your story serve you is to share it with others. Earlier we learned about the powerful hold shame has on us and how, in all its insidious evil, it isolates us from one another. We can turn loneliness around by sharing our pain and story with others. Sharing our story and what we learned from it can lift others up out of their pain.

Reaching this level of altruism defines our post-traumatic growth with resilience and grace. It also empowers us to step into the next level of our being, where we elevate ourselves mentally, emotionally, and spiritually. It is on this continued path that we will find the ultimate freedom. It is where we will ultimately rise above our story.

. . . .

LET'S SUM IT UP

When we let our story serve us, when we find the silver lining, we change the dynamic. We change our relationship with our story. We are no longer beholden to it. We aren't the victim. Instead, we look for the good that came from our pain. Perhaps it is something in your physical world: a new friend, a new job, or a move to a new city. Maybe it's an inner shift that has left you stronger or more self-aware. It is often in the unearthing of our deepest pain that we find the most resilient and beautiful parts of ourselves. We can also have our story serve us by sharing our pain with others. Shedding the cloak of shame and offering our stories to help others is one of the most powerful ways our stories can serve us.

. . . .

NOW IT'S YOUR TURN

This is where we unpack your story and see if we can find the silver lining that serves your highest being. This is such a powerful part of our journey together, so it's important that you hone in on these questions and answer them with objective honesty. Unearthing the beauty from your pain means that you refuse to be victimized by your story. It's also how you stand in your power. This is how we flip the script on your story and let it serve you.

Get comfortable and take a few slow, deep breaths. There is a part of you that craves authentic healing—a part that wants to rise above the story. When that part of you speaks of the goodness in your life that was a byproduct of your pain, tune in. That is the part of you that we want to answer these questions—that which desires your inner peace more than anything else.

As with the other journal prompts, you may choose to go through these several times so you can process more than one trauma or story, and that's perfectly okay. This is your chance to unearth as much beauty as possible. Take as much time as you need. The results will be worth it.

Describe one trauma and the resulting story your brain created because of it. (If it helps, refer to your answers in chapter 3.)

Was there a positive change in your physical environment because of this trauma? Did you move? Meet someone new? Change careers? Schools? End an unhealthy relationship?

Did you experience a positive inner shift because of the trauma or your story? Did you become stronger? Wiser? More insightful? More compassionate?

Can you accept that in some way you are better because of what happened?

Do you see that you are not what happened to you? You are the walking embodiment of grace and strength. Share three examples of how you've exhibited grace and strength in your life.

How can you use that old trauma and story to help others?

How can you use your old trauma and story to better yourself in some way?

Is there a fire in you? Some part of you that wants more? What does it want? Love, money, success, health?

Are you ready to rise above your story no matter how scary it might feel?

You did such a great job unearthing the beauty in your pain. Give yourself a big hug. Your fortitude is remarkable. I know you want ultimate healing and that includes emotional freedom and unconditional love, which is where we'll go next. Hold on, my beautiful friend, we're *this* close to finally rising above the story!

11

UNCONDITIONAL SELF-LOVE AND EMOTIONAL FREEDOM

Growing up as I did, I never believed in happy endings. I couldn't. Every time something good happened, something bad came along and squashed every iota of it. I loved getting lost in books and movies where the girl gets the guy and families sing carols around the Christmas tree, but I didn't believe anything like that could ever happen to me.

Decades later, when I was doing the work to finally rise above my story, there were days when I wondered if a happy ending might actually be in the cards for me. Then there were other days when it felt as though I'd jumped off an anchored boat tethered tightly to the ocean floor and swum halfway toward land. The boat, while certainly not a happy place, felt familiar and inviting compared to the unknown life that awaited me onshore. I had to decide whether I'd keep swimming toward a new way of life or stay anchored in my old ways.

When we do this kind of transformative inner work, there is always a tinge of melancholy for the comfort of what was and a temptation to return to it. That's completely normal. As we've learned, anxiety and chaos can feel oddly comforting. So how do we stay the course toward a life of emotional freedom?

How do we rise above our story once and for all?

We do it by learning to love ourselves unconditionally.

Up until now unconditional self-love probably felt unattainable. Before you started this Rise Above the Story work, your old trauma wound was still raw and gaping. You didn't know how to release the shame you felt around the trauma. Your emotional brain was running the show, pumping out stories to keep you "safe" and closed off from the world. And bit by bit your story entangled you in its nonsense until it ultimately took over your life. I'm here to tell you that it's difficult to love yourself when you have an emotional tsunami raging inside you.

But that's not where we are anymore. Right now, in this space, you stand with me as someone who's acknowledged their story, untangled themselves from it, and learned how powerful an untruthful story can be. You, my beautiful friend, now have a fresh, clean slate to create the life you want. And it all starts with learning to love yourself.

When I was on my own Rise Above the Story journey, I spent quite a bit of time vacillating between my old ways and my new self. I ultimately rose above my story when I learned to love every part of myself. *Every* single part. The old, the new, the shiny, and the lackluster. I even loved all the parts of me I had banished in shame. Once I tapped into that self-love, I was emotionally liberated for the first time in my life. I was no longer merely existing. I was no longer ashamed. I was self-aware. I knew how to process my emotions. And, for the first time in my life, I wasn't waiting for someone else to rescue or fix me. I could now do that all on my own. How empowering is that?

And that's what I want for you.

For most of us, especially as trauma survivors, loving ourselves doesn't come naturally. Because of what we've been through, we might default to pleasing others before we please ourselves. We most likely feel guilt and shame—a lot of it. And if we're being completely honest, it's impossible to love ourselves when we're ashamed of who we are. If you resonate with this, stay with me. You can learn to love yourself unconditionally. Here are a few ways to tap into the eternal well of love inside you.

FIND COMPASSION FOR EVERY PART OF YOURSELF

As Dr. Gabor Maté writes in his book, *The Myth of Normal: Trauma, Illness, and Healing in a Toxic Culture*, "People bearing trauma's scars almost uniformly develop a shame-based view of themselves at the core, a negative self-perception most of them are all too conscious of. Among the most poisonous consequences of shame is the loss of compassion for oneself. The more severe the trauma, the more total that loss."[71]

Indeed, due to the harrowing nature of my trauma, finding compassion for myself was the most difficult part of my self-love journey. While fueled on guilt and shame, I questioned *everything* about myself, even my professional success. It turns out that many trauma survivors achieve great success only to later question their worthiness. We drive ourselves with shame, fearful that we'll turn out like our parents or that people will find out who we *really* are, which is ironic considering *we* don't even know who we really are. But even the greatest achievements and external validation won't heal our deep pain or rewrite our stories. The temporary high we feel after succeeding only masks the shame that tortures us. Instead, it is self-compassion that will unearth our true self, but our stories of shame and unworthiness block compassion at every turn.

Our shameful stories might also cause us to shun parts of ourselves. When we feel guilty or embarrassed by something we did, we'll suppress the emotions surrounding the event lest they make us feel out of control and dirty. This often leads to us shunning or splintering off those pieces of ourselves. For me this meant shunning the six-year-old beaten-down me who switched roles with my mother and the twelve-year-old hustler me who took money from neighbors. It also meant splintering off the destitute thirteen-year-old me who went without hot water and electricity. There were countless pieces of me that I rejected and buried in a heap of shame.

We can't truly love ourselves when we splinter our being this way, so we need to bring all those parts of us back together. And we do this with compassion. Here are a few ways to fuel your self-compassion.

COMPASSION MEDITATION

Practicing compassion meditation was extremely helpful in my self-love journey. As I shared in chapter 8, I used this practice to develop a healthy relationship with my inner child, which went a long way in my quest for self-love since so much of my trauma was tied to my youth. I used this meditation to observe myself at various stages of my life, including being a caretaker to my dying mother, being a mother to my brother, reluctantly marrying Max, feeling like an imposter professionally, and feeling out of place socially. With enough time and meditation sessions, I accepted that those versions of me did their very best with what they knew at the time. In my mind's eye I comforted each of them until they no longer felt shameful, scared, and lonely.

COMPASSION LETTERS

Another powerful way to find compassion for yourself is to write a letter to the part of you that you're ashamed of. Go back to the moment that's causing you so much shame. Stand in the space. Witness yourself doing what makes you feel so ashamed today. Now think about what you knew, how you felt, and why you did what you did. Acknowledge your courage and resilience and what it took for you to endure your circumstances. Honor that part of you that carried you to the next phase of your life. You wouldn't be here today had that part of you not shown up exactly as it did. Invite that part of you back into your life with an apology for leaving it behind. And most of all, offer that hurt part of you your love and adoration.

Compassion meditation and letter writing are powerful ways to welcome back in the parts of you that you've shunned. When we compassionately accept all the parts of us with open arms, we will find love for the whole of us. You might even find that by practicing this kind, glorious compassion you've tapped into higher consciousness, that sweet space where your emotional and thinking brains find harmony.

HONOR YOUR EMOTIONS

Honoring our emotions is a crucial part of our self-love journey. When we're out of sync with ourselves, or caught up in our story, our emotions can overwhelm us. In times like these, it's easy to ignore our authentic emotions. Subconsciously it may feel like too much to deal with. Or perhaps we feel guilty for being angry, sad, or confused. For most of us, it's shame. We're ashamed to feel the way we do, so we suppress our emotions and hope they'll go away.

But remember, emotions are energy. They are meant to be felt, processed, and honored until they dissipate. In fact, the word *emotion* is derived from the Latin *emovere*, meaning to move out or away, to dislodge. Our emotional nature is meant to be one of flow. If it is not, our suppressed negative energy can fester, causing mental and emotional dis-ease and even physical disease.

So how do we get around our negative emotions? We don't. As you know by now, one of my favorite spiritual laws of healing says *the only way out is through*. Earlier, when we discussed the toll that unresolved emotional energy takes on the body, I shared with you my "I See You" method of processing emotions. Below is an expanded version of that exercise. It's a surefire method that will help you not only process those uncomfortable emotions but honor them for what value they bring you.

- First, give yourself permission, time, and space to feel the emotion. Go somewhere quiet without distraction. If that means locking yourself in the bathroom or stowing away in the closet, do it. Turn off your phone to ensure that you're focused and still.

- Next, identify your emotion with clarity, then be honest about why you feel that way. Really honest. The top note may sound like this: I'm overwhelmed with work. I'm so angry—my kids are driving me crazy. I'm frustrated that my spouse isn't helping. I lost my job, and I'm uncertain what will happen next. I slept with my ex again. I had an argument with my best friend. You get the idea.

- The next step is to unearth the deeper emotion below the top-note emotion. For instance, if your surface level emotion is anger or sadness, what's below it? Fear? Loneliness? Rejection? Disappointment? Betrayal?

- Now, dig in even deeper. It's likely that what happened triggered a deeper, unprocessed piece of your story. Why are you feeling that way? Are you afraid? Did the incident remind you of the past? Spark an insecurity? Bring out the twelve-year-old you? Whatever is causing this emotion, speak it and honor it. Loving yourself means acknowledging how you feel. You are worthy of your feelings and the time it takes to express them in a healthy and productive way.

- And now, step into your discomfort. Maybe that means taking the time to grieve your situation. It is okay to feel the loss of something that's meaningful to you (your job, your freedom, your marriage). Don't feel guilty about it. Give yourself as long as it takes to cry or feel wistful. This is a beautiful way to show yourself some love. Just like you would console a friend who was grieving, console yourself with unconditional compassion. If you're angry or rageful, do something that loosens its hold over you. Dance, jump around, yell, scream, or hit the wall with a pillow. But whatever you do here, don't get caught up in victimhood. This is about freeing yourself, not getting locked up in an emotional prison.

- Finally, when you feel the emotion has flowed through you, honor it. Imagine it floating in front of you and thank it for being there, for making you feel alive. Then, stand up, take a deep inhale, bend over at the waist, and forcefully exhale through your mouth. Stand upright and repeat, bending over and exhaling at least two more times. This breathing technique, called lion's breath, will help rid your body of whatever negative energy is left.

EMOTION JOURNAL

During my healing process, I kept an emotion journal, which is another powerful way to observe and process your emotional energy. Whenever I felt anything above or below my base level, I wrote it down and explored the circumstances and events around it. This meant I journaled about my negative *and* positive emotional energy. I wanted to learn what sent me into a dark dip and what lifted me with joy. With enough time and journaling, I saw patterns that I was able to change and embrace.

In keeping an emotion journal, you might learn that exercising gives you a boost, but too much makes you cranky. You could learn that your neighbor is an energy vampire, which triggers an old people-pleaser story in you. So now when you see her, you wave and pretend you're talking to someone on the phone. Perhaps you'll find that certain foods and drinks set you up for an emotional tidal wave. Too much gluten and alcohol throw me into an emotional tailspin for days, with old feelings of guilt and anxiety haunting my every step.

Keeping an emotion journal also helped me develop emotional competence. Coming from decades of unreconciled emotional trauma, I had to learn healthy ways to process and express my emotions. In my healing journey, my emotional pendulum swung from suppression to explosion. Even as an adult, I expected others—therapists, lovers, and friends—to fulfill my childhood emotional needs. It was crucial for my health and the health of my relationships that I learned how and when to effectively express my emotions.

In his book, *When the Body Says No*, Dr. Maté writes about the importance of emotional competence. In addition to feeling and expressing our emotions, Dr. Maté writes that emotional competence requires "the facility to distinguish between psychological reactions that are pertinent to the present situation and those that represent residue from the past. What we want and demand from the world needs to conform to our present needs, not to unconscious unsatisfied needs from childhood. If distinctions between past and present blur, we will perceive loss or the threat of loss where none exists . . ."[72] Emotional competence helps us maintain healthy expectations in relationships. With time and self-awareness, we'll know our triggers and become attuned to what is a present-moment emotional infraction versus a previously unmet childhood need.

Emotions are how we experience our humanness. They fill us with life and connect us to others. By honoring your emotions through the lens of emotional competence, you're honoring yourself. What a gift it is to feel the emotional rhythm of life. Sometimes it's fast and other times it's slow. But we must strive to keep it in sync with who we truly are: a flawed but majestically perfect being worthy of love, especially our own.

LEARN TO ENJOY YOUR OWN COMPANY

Another way to tap into your self-love is to spend time alone. You'll remember that after my breakup with Jack, I was terrified of being alone. Just the idea of it sent me into a spiral of anxiety. Being alone meant I'd have to face who I really was and finally process the traumatic experiences I'd endured. I couldn't bear it. I detested who I was and that poor, shameful place I came from. Spending time with others, especially in dysfunctional relationships, was the perfect distraction from how I felt and the work I needed to do.

When I finally acknowledged the stories I'd written for myself and the healing work that awaited me, everything shifted. I vowed to spend time alone despite its grueling nature. At first it was utter darkness. No matter what I did, I couldn't gather up enough fortitude to light the way. But through the tearful days and the sleepless nights, I kept trying. After a while, being alone got a little more comfortable, and then little by little, I found solace in my own company.

In being alone, I had created the container where I would do my most challenging work, where I would ultimately fall in love with myself and find true emotional freedom. These days I crave alone time. I relish the days that I schedule time alone to nurture myself. I tune in and ask what I need and want and then I make it happen.

Enjoying time alone is a crucial part of the self-love formula. Nurturing yourself enhances your self-esteem. Turning inward regularly is how we begin to rely on ourselves (and no one else) for our emotional strength and resilience. If this all sounds spiritually yummy yet equally terrifying, you're not alone.

Maybe you aren't used to spending time alone. Perhaps you've been a serial committer and now you're going through a divorce, or you're from a big, dysfunctional family and now you're out in the world by yourself. I've been there, too. Big life shifts can feel daunting, and if we've never tapped into self-love or felt confident in who we really are, spending time alone can be scary.

Here are a few ways to make spending time alone not only feel more comfortable but become something you crave:

- Because, as we know, self-awareness is the key to healing, it's important to acknowledge your loneliness. Sit with it. Understand it. Talk to it. If you push it away, it will come back with a vengeance, making you dislike your time alone even more. Instead, honor your loneliness for the way it makes you feel human. The goal here is to process the feeling of loneliness until it washes through you.

- What do you enjoy doing with other people? Do that alone. Eat at a restaurant. Go to the movie theater. Take a vacation. Have sex! After a while, being alone in these situations will be second nature and give you a sense of self-reliance you hadn't experienced before.

- Do meaningful things in your alone time. Bingeing Netflix is okay sometimes. But use the majority of your alone time to do things that fill you up spiritually, emotionally, mentally, and physically. Write, draw, create, play, do yoga, meditate, sign up for a new exercise class, make pottery, play the drums, go on long walks, adopt a dog. Do rewarding activities that make your alone time invaluable. Before you know it, you'll be making a date with yourself on the regular!

- Use your emotion journal and write about your inner landscape every day. With consistency and enough time, you will begin to see the subtle changes in your comfort level. You might even begin to see that your alone time is the brightest part of your day.

As a side note, enjoying your own company is also a great way to attract healthy relationships. When you come from a place of self-love, the interpersonal dynamics of your relationships will change. You will no longer *need* to be with someone just to avoid being lonely. Instead, you will choose someone as a friend or lover because you *want* them in your life. It's another huge step toward self-empowerment. Hooray!

Trust me, someday, even when you're in a healthy, loving relationship, you'll still want to sneak away and spend time alone because you'll want to reconnect with yourself. It's in this space that we check in and clean up our energy. If there's work to do, we'll work. If there's rising to do, we'll rise. Then we'll come out the other side knowing that we're enough (in fact, we're more than enough) and that we're worthy of every good thing life can offer.

STOP BEING SO MEAN TO YOURSELF

It's hard to tap into self-love when you're constantly criticizing yourself. Believe me, I get it! Some of us, myself included, are recovering perfectionists. We easily see our flaws. Heck, sometimes that's all we see. In my most perfectionist of states, I was known to drive myself to "success" by spewing insults over my inner landscape. Nothing used to make me achieve more than calling myself a few names and topping it with a catastrophic (and completely illogical) threat of failure.

Our negative self-talk may also stem from childhood. If our parents constantly pushed us to do more or be more, we can be left feeling less than well into adulthood. And some of us, due to our trauma-induced survival mode, may see potential threats at every turn, resulting in constant negativity brewing inside us.

Negative self-talk can take many forms. It can involve name-calling, ruminating, self-doubt, and self-sabotage. It may also present itself as a magnification of the negative, personalization of problems and events, and my personal favorite—imposter syndrome. There are countless successful, brilliant people in the world who go through life feeling like frauds. They're convinced they'll be found out for being unworthy of the job they have or the relationship they're in. Sound familiar?

For decades I'd talk smack about myself, to myself, and sometimes to whoever would listen. But it was the incessant, negative chatter in my head that caused me the most angst. I wasn't smart enough, pretty enough, or worthy of any job or relationship. What are some of the worst things you say about yourself? Think of three. Now imagine saying them to your best friend.

You're fat.

You're stupid.

Nobody wants to date you.

What? Would you ever? I didn't think so. Then why do we do it to ourselves? Because we haven't tapped into self-love. I know this is a little bit of a "what came first, the chicken or the egg" scenario—we talk negatively because we don't love ourselves, yet we don't love ourselves because we talk negatively. But we can stop the cycle if we understand how our brains work.

Our negative self-talk is as habitual as nail-biting or smoking. When we talk poorly about ourselves repeatedly over time, we create a pattern that, in turn, creates a neural pathway in our brain. The more we talk negatively about ourselves, the deeper and more ingrained the neural pathway becomes. With even more repetition, the signaling between brain cells in the pathway becomes faster and the negative self-talk more automatic. This pathway creates a destructive loop of self-talk that plays continually. It's like circuitry hardwired in our bodies. But here's the truth: We can kick the habit of negative self-talk just like we can any other bad habit. Here's how we do it.

- *Every day, look in the mirror and say three things you like about yourself.* This might make you feel uneasy at first, so start out simple. Maybe it's that you have a nice laugh or your right big toe looks cute today. Then you can gradually move on to deeper things, such as your quick wit, big heart, or effortless grace. But whatever you do, make it a habit. Maybe it's after you brush your teeth or before you take a shower. But be sure to look right at yourself in the mirror when you do it. Eye contact is a powerful way to connect to others and an even more powerful way to connect with yourself.

- *Cancel it out.* You want to reset the programmed circuitry of your brain so when you catch yourself saying something negative, say, "cancel" three times. Then, say the opposite of your negative self-talk, which may be, "You're so beautiful," "You're brilliant," or, "You are worthy!"

- *Focus on the positive instead of the negative.* Take ten to twenty seconds and soak in something good about yourself or something good that happened to you. Let it wash over and through you before leaving the moment. Later, when you think of something negative, remind yourself of this moment of focused good energy.

- *Talk to yourself the way you talk to your dog or cat.* This one's for all you animal lovers out there. Think about how you talk to your dog or cat. If someone recorded the way I talk to my dog, it would sound something like: "You're amazing! You're the most magnificent soul. You're adorable. You're so smart and cuddly and beautiful." This is how we talk to someone we love unconditionally. What if we spoke to ourselves that way? Can you imagine? It sounds funny and kind of uncomfortable, right? But give it a try. There's magic in the kind of love we show animals. I'm convinced they are here to teach us what we need to know, and that includes how to love ourselves.

These exercises are all about doing a hard reset of your brain circuitry and creating new inner dialogue that's nutritious and vibrant. Because the truth is we're all imperfectly perfect. Every one of us was put here to teach, create, share, and love. That's the loop we need playing in our heads, not all this negative self-talk. Can you imagine living in a body where you feel loved all the time? It's absolutely possible, and you can do it all by yourself.

CELEBRATE YOUR WINS

This is such an important facet of self-love. And, by the way, it's one that I only started myself a couple of years ago. Celebrating our wins is how we high-five ourselves. It's how we say congrats on a job well done. When's the last time you did that? If you're anything like I used to be, you skim right over your wins and move on to the next thing you must accomplish. This behavior likely stems from our trauma.

Because of the shame we carry, we may avoid the spotlight at all costs, questioning who we are to receive accolades. Due to our trauma, we might also become emotionally programmed to celebrate others yet never celebrate ourselves. Some of us might falsely believe that the win we worked so hard for was merely due to luck, while the perfectionists among us forget the good they just did and instead drive hard to the next goal. We might mistakenly believe that the faster we go and the more we accomplish, the less likely we'll be found out for who we *really* are.

If any of this resonates with you, you're not alone. So many of us don't take the time to bask in the glow of our success. We minimize our hard work and don't acknowledge how good or smart or accomplished we really are. Learning how to celebrate your wins—no matter how big or small—is a beautiful and powerful way to fuel love for yourself.

Here's how we do it:

- *Acknowledge your wins.* We must cultivate an awareness around our success (just as we did around our stories and emotions). Step outside your situation and observe your fortitude, intelligence, kindness, patience, discipline, and how hard you worked.

- *Describe how this makes you feel.* Do you feel happy? Elated? Ecstatic? Proud? Amazing? Triumphant?

- *Do something to celebrate.* Go on a bike ride. Open the bubbly. Call your bestie and brag on yourself. Take the time to honor your accomplishment.

Some days celebrating yourself may mean high-fiving yourself for getting out of bed, scheduling an appointment with a therapist, or meditating for exactly two minutes. And that's all worthy and wonderful. Every bit of momentum forward in your healing journey is worth celebrating. We're all unique in our pain and what it will take to ultimately rise above our story. Start where you are and honor every single step forward.

PRACTICE GRATITUDE

This is one of my favorite rituals because it's one of the quickest and most powerful ways to show yourself some love. When you're feeling less than, like nothing is working for you and you don't know how it can get worse, grab your journal and write down three things you're grateful for. Depending on how deep you are in the doldrums, this might feel impossible. But trust me, it's not.

Close your eyes. Inhale and exhale a few times. Think about God or the Universe shining a bright light through your heart. It feels warm and loving. When you're ready, open your eyes and write the first things that come to mind. It's beautiful (and rewarding) to write about the things *around* you that you're grateful for—your job, family, home, or dog. But I want you to go deeper and look inward.

Write one thing about your body that you're grateful for.
(I have two legs. My iron stomach. My gorgeous butt.)

Write one thing about your mind that you're grateful for.
(I'm smart. I'm funny. I'm calm under pressure.)

Write the thing you love most about yourself.
(I'm great at pickleball. I'm a speed reader. I have keen intuition.)

Doesn't that feel great? When we fall into the woe-is-me trap, there's so much we take for granted. Odds are there are countless amazing things to be grateful for. Tuning into them will remind us that we're worthy of our own love.

Another incredible practice I use several times a week is expressing gratitude for what is yet to come. I learned about this emotional resonance/quantum physics technique from Dr. Joe Dispenza's guided meditation *Reconditioning the Body to a New Mind*. In this practice, you feel gratitude for what you want to happen as if it's already occurred. If you really tap into it, you can see it, feel it, and taste it. Elation, wonder, and gratitude will wash through you over and over. I cry tears of joy every time I do Dr. Dispenza's powerful meditation. The connection it gives me to the Universe and myself is unparalleled. You must give it a try! When you teach your body to *feel* gratitude, loving yourself will become effortless.

. . . .

Once you fall in love with yourself, you'll feel more at home in the world. Being confident with who you are will foster magical opportunities for personal growth and relationships. Loving ourselves also demystifies the idea of "fitting in." Once we accept who we really are, fitting into societal structures will no longer be a priority. Instead, we'll see that being our truest, freest self means venturing beyond what is inherently comfortable into what feels excitingly like kismet. It's in these moments of exponential growth that we'll realize we're the hero we've been waiting for all along. We can climb treacherous terrain and sail the stormiest seas. With our inner compass as our guide, there is nowhere we can't navigate.

On this expedition of self-love, you'll also fully invest in your life and relationships with purposeful vulnerability. You'll want to share the deepest parts of yourself because self-love opens the floodgates of compassion. When you rise above your story, you'll be on a crusade to lovingly tell others that they can rise above their stories, too, and that they are worthy of everything they desire, including self-love.

How different the world could be if we all loved ourselves unconditionally. We'd no longer be confined by our old, limiting stories. We'd see the beauty in ourselves and others. There'd be no judgment of someone or their actions because we'd inherently know that their story is the byproduct of their pain. Compassion would be our emotional currency and love as abundant as oxygen. We'd never accept less because we'd know we're here in this life to experience more—and loving ourselves always means more. In the deep well of our being, we'd find more happiness, joy, and freedom than we ever thought possible.

Oh! And just in case you're wondering, even after rising above my story, I still don't believe in happy endings . . .

. . . because there really are no endings. There are only beginnings.

LET'S SUM IT UP

Learning to love ourselves unconditionally is the final step in rising above the story. While it can be challenging for trauma survivors to find self-love, it is possible. To tap into it, we must find compassion for each part of us, especially the parts that we've disavowed in shame. Bringing all the wounded parts and pieces of us back into the fold is necessary if we're going to find love for the whole of us. We can also find self-love by:

- honoring our emotions
- enjoying our own company
- ceasing negative self-talk
- celebrating our wins
- practicing gratitude

There is a well of love inside us that will light the path of our newly found emotional freedom.

NOW IT'S YOUR TURN

I hope at this point you're basking in the glow of your new relationship—the one with yourself. I shared the surefire ways you can tap into that reservoir of love anytime. And just like any other relationship, you'll need to foster this one, too. There'll be days when self-love is second nature, while other days will feel more challenging. Those are the moments when I want you to spend quality time with yourself. Re-read this chapter and remind yourself of how far you've come and what self-love and emotional freedom mean to you. If you need a jump start, here are a few quick questions to get you going in the right direction:

Is there a part of you still left behind in your story? A part you're ashamed of? What would you say or write to that part of yourself?

Are you shunning a part of yourself? Why?

What triggered it?

Is it based on a present need or an unresolved childhood wound?

Instead of ignoring it, can you honor it?

Can you offer that part of you love and invite it back in?

Are you suppressing any emotions? Which ones? Anger? Fear? Sadness?

What's something you enjoy doing alone that has meaning to you? Volunteering? Creating? Baking? Writing? Painting? Reading?

Will you set aside an hour today and do that?

What three things do you love most about yourself right now?

Go look at yourself in the mirror and say them to your reflection. Remember, eye contact makes it all the more powerful.

What are three things you accomplished this week? (Remember small wins are still wins!)

What did you do to celebrate? (If you didn't celebrate, stop everything immediately and high-five yourself, do a jig, or pop the bubbly!)

Share one thing about your body that you're grateful for.

Share one thing about your mind that you're grateful for.

Who's the person you're most grateful for?

Now, give yourself a hug and meet me in the next chapter. We're crossing the finish line together, my brave friend.

12

. . . .

HOW TO KEEP RISING

Congratulations! You've reached the pinnacle of your Rise Above the Story journey. You're now standing on the mountaintop, feeling the warmth of the Universe shining on you, and you're radiating the strength you've earned. It's been a difficult journey, I know. It's never easy to relinquish our old, limiting stories, especially the ones that have been with us for so long. But you did it! You've done some of the hardest work there is in this life. I hope you'll celebrate yourself, your newfound awareness, and all you've accomplished.

Our well-cultivated self-awareness is needed now more than ever because, you see, all this success doesn't mean we can rest on our laurels. To the contrary, living a fully expressed life, one of self-love and limitless emotional freedom, requires us to *continually* rise above our stories. Story creation, and the negativity that comes with it, is sadly the default mindset for most of us. Me included! I'm a fixer and a people pleaser by default. Perhaps you are, too? And let me just say that healing is a lifelong process. While we can indeed heal our deepest wounds and rewrite our most painful stories, situations will inevitably arise that might lure us into our old stories.

But don't be discouraged.

Shifting into old mindsets is part of being human. Everyone has, at one time or another, slipped back into old patterns. But here's where you and I and all those other Risers out there are different. We've shifted out of the emotional brain into the thinking brain. We've cultivated an awareness of our default story settings. We're cognizant of triggers. We think twice before crossing emotional landmines. With this awareness, we must remain vigilant and walk through life with keen awareness so we don't get caught up in our old, negative stories or, worse yet, create new ones.

How do we know if we're on the cusp of relapsing? One surefire way is to tune into your body. What's happening when these old stories are festering? Is your stomach churning? Is your heart beating faster? Is your mood suddenly dark? Are your palms clammy? Is your mind spinning? Do you feel anger or rage? Do you drop out or disassociate from life? When these alarms go off, you'll know that your emotional brain is fired up. That's when it's time to call upon our tried-and-true Rise Above the Story formula:

1. *Acknowledge the story.* Identify the trauma (or the trigger for an old trauma) and then using objective, factual language, describe the trauma and the story. Remember to be completely honest about what you're telling yourself. How is the story limiting your life, dreams, and relationships? How is it keeping you small?

2. *Release the story.* Start by untangling yourself from the story. Ask yourself: Where did it come from? What triggered you? Is it an old pattern or a new fear? What emotions are you feeling? Anger? Shame? Fear? What is the emotional parallel between how you felt historically and how you feel now? Next, extract your true self. Remember that you are not your story. Does your inner child need some love? Can you forgive someone? Do you need to forgive yourself? Is there a silver lining that can be unearthed?

3. *Rise above the story.* Tap into unconditional self-love. Find compassion for yourself. Honor your emotions. Spend time alone doing something that fills you up. Be kind to yourself. Celebrate your wins. Be grateful for your self-awareness. Know that you are enough. That you are limitless. That you are worthy of love, especially your own.

NEW OPPORTUNITIES TO RISE

While we'll continue rising above our old stories, we'll also have plenty of opportunities to rise above new stories. With enough practice (and success!), we'll see life's curveballs not only as opportunities to rise again but gifts that enable us to rise even higher than before. In our lifetime, there will be more than one story that plagues us and more than one opportunity to rise. There will, and should, be countless opportunities to

rise above our stories. This is how we grow and experience a rich, meaningful life. It's how we expand our being and fill our soul with wisdom.
This is why we must never be afraid of rising. Instead, we should see it as
a blessing, a moment when the Universe's spotlight is shining on us, so
we can once again rise to a new level of strength, love, and compassion.

I've had, and continue to have, countless opportunities to rise. One
powerful situation offered me exponential spiritual growth. When Jack
lit me up with desire while I was still married to Max, I glimpsed for
the first time that I was worthy of my feelings. For years, I'd shut down
emotionally and physically. I didn't feel anything except numb. But
being with Jack sparked a fire in me I didn't know existed. Even before
we had sex, just the thought of him made dormant parts of me throb with
wanting—I wanted more for me and for my life.

We all know what happened with Jack and how losing him gutted me.
But in retrospect, I now see that the real reason I met Jack wasn't about
sex or even Jack himself. It was about the Universe offering me the chance
to rise on multiple levels. Loving Jack (and his crazy, hot bravado) was
the jolt I needed to restart my life. I had been languishing in a passionless
marriage, constantly scanning restaurants for my soulmate while at dinner
with my husband. I deserved more. And so did Max. Jack erupted in me
a passion for more, and for the first time in my life I felt worthy of rising.
And so I did. I allowed myself to finally feel, emote, and love.

The end of my relationship with Jack was also the beginning of
rising above my story. It was in those days of panicked anxiety that I
began therapy and dove deep into my past. With enough time, I moved
emotionally beyond Jack. I wasn't ready yet to fully rise above my story,
but I held sacred my desire for a more vibrant life. For the first time, I
believed I was worthy of more than I'd had. I wanted my relationships
to be richer, especially the one I had with myself.

I rose above my lifelong story of worthlessness incrementally. I knew I was worthy of feeling exhilaration, passion, and desire, and I did it with no shame. I learned that I didn't have to be numb to survive. I could share parts of me that felt safe yet exciting, while the rest of me remained stowed away waiting for another opportunity to rise to an even higher realm of emotional awareness and healing.

While relationships often offer us our richest and most multifaceted opportunities to rise, our professional journeys, and even more so our quest for purpose, can lead us into a sea of opportunities. After Mom died, I began my legal career. I needed a solid career that could support Brandon and me. Sounds like rising, right? It most certainly was. I mustered every bit of resilience I had and rose above the poverty-stricken, defeated life I knew.

I let my story serve me.

That version of life I rose to—being a criminal trial lawyer—didn't fill me up and I wasn't truly happy, but it was the next step—the level up—from where I'd been my whole life. And it was enough. Until it wasn't. Again, I wanted more. I'd ignored my desires for a fuller life, a more meaningful career, a richer purpose because I didn't believe I was worthy of such things. Being a lawyer was what I knew. I didn't even know what else I wanted to do, but I knew what I was doing wasn't enough. My unease grew more each day. I'd meet up with other lawyers for happy hour and exchange the obligatory *you won't believe what happened* stories over draft beers. When all the stories started sounding the same and my pants went up two sizes, I wondered if maybe the jig was up. Was it finally time to change careers? To do something that fueled my passion and purpose?

But before I could rise again, I had to go deep. I had to acknowledge my story and extract my truth. I had to get real about who I was in my current story (successful lawyer but longing for something more person-ally purposeful) and why I wrote my story of unworthiness.

Was I brave enough to let go of my limiting story? Yes. But it took me a few more years to find my purpose and the mindset shift where it didn't feel like I was giving up anything. In fact, in those moments of healing, when my gargantuan trauma wounds were on the mend, I knew it was time to shift into my purpose with confidence and grace. I no longer cared what others thought of me or my decisions. And when I finally felt worthy of my dreams, I fulfilled my needs and desires with-out shame or guilt.

At long last, I'd found emotional freedom.

The Universe challenged me again a few years later, when Irwin, a dog I'd grown to love so deeply that I called him "the furry love of my life," was diagnosed with cancer. He's from the same lineage as Finn, but genealogy aside, I knew this was the Universe checking in to make sure I'd truly risen above my story of abandonment. Would his diagnosis send me into a tizzy of wounded victimhood, or would I find the grace in what was transpiring? I allowed myself a few days to grieve the situation and to be furious that this was happening again.

After the waves of grief and anger dissipated, I was awash with a deep knowing. I knew that this was part of my journey, part of Irwin's journey, and part of our mission here together. I knew that no matter what happened, we'd be okay. I also saw it as a gift; this diagnosis was a chance for me to feel gratitude for the time we shared instead of tak-ing for granted time that is promised to no one. I chose to honor Irwin with the best integrative health protocol for the remainder of his Earth journey, however long that was, and to love him every second of every day until his angels came for him. I rested in knowing that he would never really leave me just as Finn didn't. Because now I know that when someone loves you, they never really leave you.

. . . .

Rising above our story is not linear, and it is never, *ever* a one and done. Unfortunately, the cruelest stories are the hardest to rid ourselves of. From time to time, they'll poke around, looking to stir up trouble. There will also be multiple layers to rising and plenty of opportunities to rise above new stories. Instead of being fearful, we must look at each situation as an opportunity to grow and achieve what we most desire. You're already ahead of the game because you know the Rise Above the Story formula—*acknowledge the story, release the story, and rise above the story*. You now have a lifelong tool of empowerment that will all but ensure you'll find peace and love in yourself first and always.

What I know for sure is that like a phoenix, we will be set ablaze countless times in our lives, but it is our ascension from the ashes in a blaze of bold color that is the ultimate rising. We aren't here to suffer or live in the past. We aren't here to write sad, untrue stories. We're here to rise again and again until we ultimately reach the heavens.

And there, with love and the warmth of the sun, the Universe will honor us for our work well done.

Work well done, indeed.

LOVE LETTER TO THE READER

When you need a reminder of your worthiness
or how much you are loved, return to this page.

D ear Beautiful Soul,
You have done what many say is impossible—you've risen above your story. You now know that everything you need is inside you. You have heart and fortitude. You have immeasurable strength and courage. You are the epitome of grace and compassion. Now is the time to bask in the swell of what's possible for you and live a limitless life free of shame and fear.

Undoubtedly, there will be cloudy days ahead, but the unconditional love you have for yourself will steer you toward the sun. You are worthy and must now wholeheartedly accept and expect the good that life bestows upon you. Gratitude for these blessings goes without saying because it is in these moments of thankfulness that we spiritually resonate with the joy of today instead of the pain of yesterday.

May this simple yet powerful Rise Above the Story formula lift you higher each day. This book, and all of its teachings, are here for you now and always.

And so am I.

With resilience and love,

Karena

ACKNOWLEDGMENTS

I can't believe I'm here! *Here*, to the acknowledgments—to the end of a long journey of writing and editing. But also, *here*—alive, empowered, and healed. I wouldn't have made it *here* had it not been for the beautiful, loving people I thank below.

David, my lover, my constant companion, my North Star. Thank you for keeping me on course with your steadfast devotion. I could never have made it *here* without your unwavering love and support.

To Brandon, Jessica, and Jackson. Thank you for the gift of motherhood. May you feel forever nurtured and loved. You are worthy of all that and more.

Kaisa, you are my chosen family. You encouraged my dreams and nurtured me when I was ready to give up. For all that and more, I love you.

Jodi, there's not enough gratitude in the world for all the sidewalk healing we did together. No matter the distance between us, you're always in my heart.

Steve Harris, you are the agent of agents. Thank you for championing my cause.

To my editor Rachel Phares, you have my gratitude for tirelessly tweaking my manuscript. We left some juicy sections on the cutting room floor, but my book is undoubtedly better because of your keen eye.

My thanks to the BenBella publishing team and a special shout-out to Sarah Avinger for indulging our over one hundred emails to ensure that my vision for the Holi-inspired book cover came to life.

Richelle Fredson, the book proposal work we did blazed my path. For that and more, you have my gratitude.

Thanks to Michelle Garside. The work you do makes the world a better place.

To all my healers—the words on these pages would not have flourished without your wisdom.

Cheryl, for all the organic love and enlightenment, I am forever grateful. You are and always will be my spirit mother.

To Debbie for teaching me that I have the power to heal myself, and to Linda for tending to my wounds with stardust. Undoubtedly, I've loved you both in this lifetime and many others before.

To all the dogs who've loved me. You bestowed on me the weighted comfort of unconditional love and the unbearable agony of loss. May we meet again at the rainbow bridge.

To the believers, dreamers, and doers who found themselves in the pages of this book. We've always been one—aligned in our trauma; but now, we're united in our rising. Here's to you for believing in yourself. I am so incredibly proud of you.

And last, but certainly not least, to me—for being *here,* for ridding myself of shame, and for rising above my story.

NOTES

1   "Effects," The National Child Traumatic Stress Network, March 23, 2018, https://www.nctsn.org/what-is-child-trauma/trauma-types/early-childhood-trauma/effects.

2   Gabor Maté, *The Myth of Normal: Trauma, Illness, and Healing in a Toxic Culture* (New York: Avery, 2022), 141.

3   Ibid.

4   Ibid.

5   Bruce D. Perry and Oprah Winfrey, *What Happened to You: Conversations on Trauma, Resilience, and Healing* (New York: Flatiron Books, 2021), 31.

6   "Understanding Child Trauma," SAMHSA, n.d. https://www.samhsa.gov/child-trauma/understanding-child-trauma.

7   "How to Manage Trauma," The National Council, accessed June 7, 2023, https://www.thenationalcouncil.org/wp-content/uploads/2022/08/Trauma-infographic.pdf.

8   Ibid.

9   "Post-Traumatic Stress Disorder (PTSD)," National Institute of Mental Health (NIMH), n.d. https://www.nimh.nih.gov/health/statistics/post-traumatic-stress-disorder-ptsd.

10   Dr. Dan Siegel, "Dr. Dan Siegel's Hand Model of the Brain," YouTube video, August 9, 2017, 0:33, www.youtube.com/watch?v=f-m2YcdMdFw&t=27s.

11   Daniel Siegel, *Mindsight: The New Science of Personal Transformation* (New York: Bantam Books Trade Paperbacks, 2010), 15–16.

12   Dr. Dan Siegel, "Dr. Dan Siegel's Hand Model of the Brain," YouTube video, August 9, 2017, 3:52, www.youtube.com/watch?v=f-m2YcdMdFw&t=27s.

13   Siegel, *Mindsight*, 17.

14   Ibid., 16–17.

15 Bessel van der Kolk, *The Body Keeps the Score: Brain, Mind, and Body in the Healing of Trauma* (New York: Penguin Books, 2015), 57.

16 Dr. Dan Siegel, "Dr. Dan Siegel's Hand Model of the Brain," YouTube video, August 9, 2017, 4:55, www.youtube.com/watch?v=f-m2YcdMdFw&t=27s.

17 Siegel, *Mindsight,* 21.

18 Ibid.

19 Amanda S. Hodel, "Rapid Infant Prefrontal Cortex Development and Sensitivity to Early Environmental Experience," *Developmental Review* 48 (2018): 113–44, https://doi.org/10.1016/j.dr.2018.02.003.

20 Mariam Arain et al., "Maturation of the Adolescent Brain," *Neuropsychiatric Disease and Treatment* 9 (2013): 449–61, https://doi.org/10.2147/NDT.S39776.

21 van der Kolk, *The Body Keeps the Score*, 57.

22 Dr. Dan Siegel, "Dr. Dan Siegel's Hand Model of the Brain," YouTube video, August 9, 2017, 5:38, www.youtube.com/watch?v=f-m2YcdMdFw&t=27s.

23 Maté, *The Myth of Normal*, 125–26.

24 Professional, Cleveland Clinic Medical, "Nervous System," Cleveland Clinic, accessed June 29, 2023, https://my.clevelandclinic.org/health/articles/21202-nervous-system.

25 Professional, Cleveland Clinic Medical, "Somatic Nervous System," Cleveland Clinic, accessed June 29, 2023, https://my.clevelandclinic.org/health/body/23291-somatic-nervous-system.

26 Professional, Cleveland Clinic Medical, "Autonomic Nervous System," Cleveland Clinic, accessed June 29, 2023, https://my.clevelandclinic.org/health/body/23273-autonomic-nervous-system.

27 Cassandra Holloway, "What Happens to Your Body During the Fight-or-Flight Response?" *Cleveland Clinic* (blog), April 7, 2023, https://health.clevelandclinic.org/what-happens-to-your-body-during-the-fight-or-flight-response/.

28 Perry and Winfrey, *What Happened to You*, 59.

29 "Trauma and the Freeze Response: Good, Bad, or Both?" Psychology Today, accessed June 7, 2023, https://www.psychologytoday.com/us/blog/evolution-the-self/201507/trauma-and-the-freeze-response-good-bad-or-both.

30 Professional, Cleveland Clinic Medical, "Sympathetic Nervous System (SNS)," Cleveland Clinic, accessed June 7, 2023, http://www.my.clevelandclinic.org/health/body/23262-sympathetic-nervous-system-sns-fight-or-flight.

31 Perry and Winfrey, *What Happened to You*, 37.

32 Ibid., 61.

33 Siegel, *Mindsight*, 17.

34 van der Kolk, *The Body Keeps the Score*, 32.

35 Ibid.

36 Maté, *The Myth of Normal*, 77.

37 Vincent J. Felitti, MD, FACP et al., "Relationship of Childhood Abuse and Household Dysfunction to Many of the Leading Causes of Death in

Adults," *American Journal of Preventive Medicine* 14, no. 4 (1998): 245–58. https://doi.org/10.1016/s0749-3797(98)00017-8.
38   Ibid.
39   Maté, *The Myth of Normal*, 92–93.
40   van der Kolk, *The Body Keeps the Score*, 46.
41   Gabor Maté, *When the Body Says No: Exploring the Stress-Disease Connection* (New Jersey: John Wiley & Sons, Inc., 2003), 61.
42   Ibid.
43   Kelly A. Turner, *Radical Remission: Surviving Cancer Against All Odds* (New York: Harper One, 2015), 144.
44   Arlin Cuncic, MA, "Holotropic Breathwork Benefits and Risks," Verywell Mind, May 2013, https://www.verywellmind.com/holotropic-breathwork-4175431.
45   "Controlling the Autonomic Nervous System," Wim Hof Method, n.d., https://www.wimhofmethod.com/controlling-the-autonomic-nervous-system.
46   "Meditation: A Simple, Fast Way to Reduce Stress," Mayo Clinic, April 29, 2022, http://www.mayoclinic.org/tests-procedures/meditation/in-depth/meditation/art-20045858.
47   Ibid.
48   John Horton, "Infrared Saunas: What They Do and 6 Health Benefits," *Cleveland Clinic* (blog), April 14, 2022, https://health.clevelandclinic.org/infrared-sauna-benefits/.
49   Tanjaniina Laukkanen, Jari A. Laukkanen, and Setor K. Kunutsor, "Sauna Bathing and Risk of Psychotic Disorders: A Prospective Cohort Study," *Medical Principles and Practice* 27, no. 6 (2018): 562–69. https://doi.org/10.1159/000493392.
50   "What Is Tapping and How Does It Work?" Tapping Solution Foundation, n.d., https://www.tappingsolutionfoundation.org/howdoesitwork/.
51   Ibid.
52   van der Kolk, *The Body Keeps the Score,* 209.
53   "What Is EMDR?" EMDR Institute, Inc., https://www.emdr.com/what-is-emdr/.
54   Ibid.
55   Christina Caron, "This Nerve Influences Nearly Every Internal Organ. Can It Improve Our Mental State, Too?" *The New York Times*, June 2, 2022, https://www.nytimes.com/2022/06/02/well/mind/vagus-nerve-mental-health.html.
56   Ibid.
57   Ibid.
58   Douglas J. Bremner et al., "Transcutaneous Cervical Vagal Nerve Stimulation in Patients with Posttraumatic Stress Disorder (PTSD): A Pilot Study of Effects on PTSD Symptoms and Interleukin-6 Response to Stress," *Journal of Affective Disorders Reports* 6 (December 2021): 100190, https://doi.org/10.1016/j.jadr.2021.100190.
59   "Vagus Nerve Stimulation (VNS)," Cleveland Clinic, n.d., https://my.clevelandclinic.org/health/treatments/17598-vagus-nerve-stimulation.

60 Perishable, "SE 101," Somatic Experiencing® International, March 23, 2021, http://www.traumahealing.org/se-101/.

61 Ibid.

62 Traci Pedersen, "Can Hypnotherapy Help with Trauma?" Psych Central, September 19, 2022, https://www.psychcentral.com/health/hypnotherapy-trauma #how-hypnotherapy-works.

63 Assen Alladin and Alisha Alibhai, "Cognitive Hypnotherapy for Depression: *An Empirical Investigation*," *International Journal of Clinical and Experimental Hypnosis* 55, no. 2 (2007): 147–66, https://doi.org/10.1080/00207140601177897.

64 Perry and Winfrey, *What Happened to You*, 49.

65 "Dr. Bruce Perry Interview – Rhythmic Mind," February 5, 2019, https://www .rhythmicmind.net/2019/02/05/dr-bruce-perry-interview/.

66 van der Kolk, *The Body Keeps the Score*, 216.

67 "The 4 Functions of Rhythm in Expressive Arts Therapy," Psychology Today, accessed June 7, 2023, https://www.psychologytoday.com/us/blog/arts-and-health /202011/the-4-functions-rhythm-in-expressive-arts-therapy.

68 "How Dogs Can Help with Depression," NAMI: National Alliance on Mental Illness, n.d., https://www.nami.org/Blogs/NAMI-Blog/February-2018/How-Dogs -Can-Help-with-Depression.

69 Andrea Beetz et al., "Psychosocial and Psychophysiological Effects of Human-Animal Interactions: The Possible Role of Oxytocin," *Frontiers in Psychology* 3 (July 2012), https://doi.org/10.3389/fpsyg.2012.00234.

70 Jérémy Daniel and Margaret Haberman, "Clinical Potential of Psilocybin as a Treatment for Mental Health Conditions," *The Mental Health Clinician* 7, no. 1 (2017): 24–28, https://doi.org/10.9740/mhc.2017.01.024.

71 Maté, *The Myth of Normal*, 30.

72 Maté, *When the Body Says No*, 38.

ABOUT THE AUTHOR

Karena Kilcoyne is a former criminal defense attorney turned author. When she's not loving dogs or helping others rise above their stories, she's curating a colorful life of books and art from far-flung places. Karena lives in Florida with her husband David and their furry son Irwin.

Photo by Wolf Marloh